THE MATCHY MATCHY SEWING BOOK

THE MATCHY MATCHY SEWING BOOK

FLEXIBLE, FUN, AND SATISFYING SEWING PROJECTS USING SIMPLE SHAPES

Amy Gonzales and Theresa Kuo

Countryman Press

An Imprint of W. W. Norton & Company
Independent Publishers Since 1923

Printed in China
First American Edition 2025

For information about permission to reproduce selections from this book, write to Permissions, Countryman Press, 500 Fifth Avenue, New York, NY 10110

For information about special discounts for bulk purchases, please contact W. W. Norton Special Sales at specialsales@wwnorton.com or 800-233-4830

Countryman Press
www.countrymanpress.com

An imprint of W. W. Norton & Company, Inc.
500 Fifth Avenue, New York, NY 10110
www.wwnorton.com

Conceived, edited, and designed by Quarto Publishing, an imprint of The Quarto Group
1 Triptych Place, London SE1 9SH

QUAR.1179378

Commissioning editor: Anna Galkina
Assistant editor: Ella Whiting
Copy editor: Marie Clayton
Cover and layout designer: Hello Daly
Art director: Martina Calvio
Photographers: Leanne Jade (cover and model photography), Amy Gonzales and Theresa Kuo (lifestyle, flatlay, and cover photography)
Stylist: Claire Montgomerie
Production manager: David Hearn
Managing editor: Emma Harverson
Publisher: Lorraine Dickey

978-1-68268-991-2

1 2 3 4 5 6 7 8 9 0

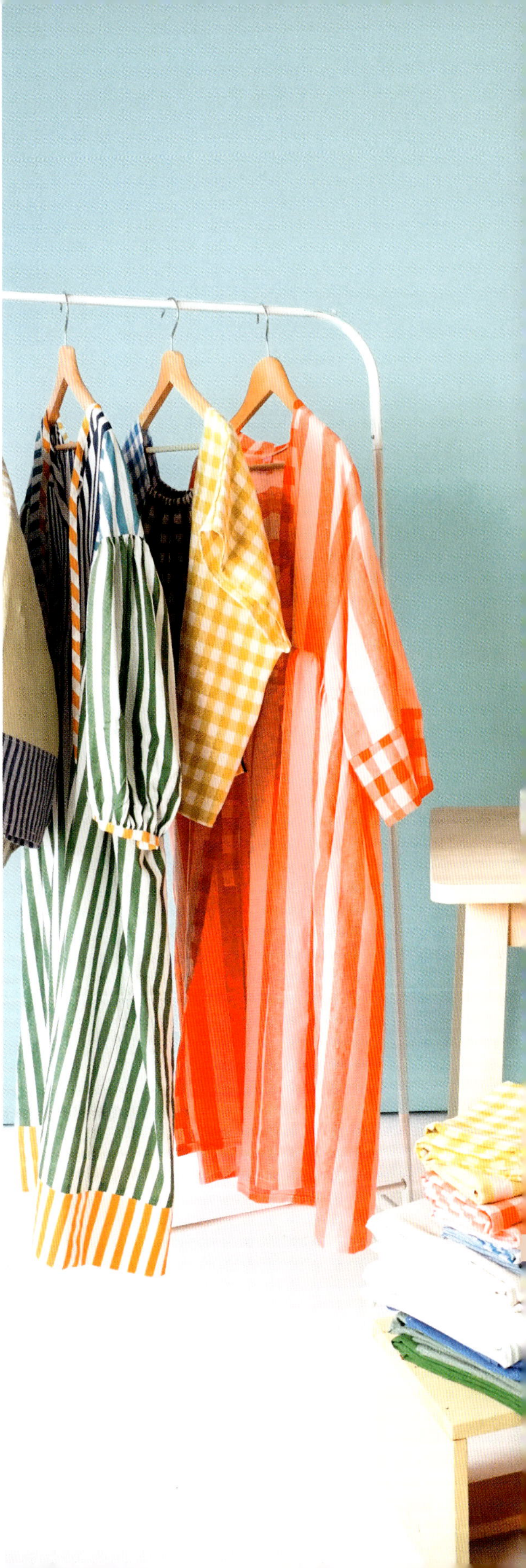

CONTENTS

WELCOME TO THE CLUB!

As self-taught sewists who believe that creativity doesn't have to be complicated, we're always dreaming up beginner-friendly, design-forward ways to make the whole creative experience of sewing simple, satisfying, and so fun. In this step-by-step guide you will learn skill-building techniques to guide you through any project. Whether you lean toward minimalism, maximalism, or anywhere in between, you will come away with garments that fit your style and funnel your creativity into a wearable closet based on straightforward silhouettes and the Matchy Scrap Theory. We're on a mission to help you have as much fun making your garments as you do wearing them.

Organized into two parts, this book begins with a simple explanation of our process and theory of making based on easy patterns, mixing, matching, and using what you've got. This part also explores the basic tools you need to set up a dreamy workroom, how to find your desired fit, and easy-to-understand techniques needed for sewing any garment. The second section showcases 12 sewing projects, with nine garment patterns in sizes XXS–6XL and three fun accessories. The projects are organized so that they build confidence as you learn new skills using the simply shaped pattern pieces; and the Matchy Scrap Theory guides you to select fabrics that mix and match to their fullest potential. Each project is clearly demonstrated with step-by-step illustrations and has a downloadable PDF pattern that can be accessed via the QR code on page 22. This is your invitation to grab what you've got, make it your own, and enjoy the process.

THE PROCESS AND THEORY OF MAKING

SCRAP THEORY

Scrap theory is our own term for the alchemy that happens when small scraps of different colors and patterns combine into a larger, more intricate design. The result is a unique creation that's even more stunning than its individual parts. It's part art form, part color science, and all magic.

At Matchy Matchy, we always keep scrap theory in mind when designing our sewing patterns. We love the way colors and patterns can come together to create truly unique and personal looks. These one-of-a-kind pieces often have a story behind each fabric scrap, adding to their charm. Our patterns are designed with simplicity in mind, using straightforward shapes and minimal pieces, with clear lines or panels that offer endless patchwork possibilities.

We often hear that the most fun and challenging part of scrap theory is choosing the fabric combination. Our advice? Don't stress over it. You don't need to know the exact outcome when you begin. Overplanning or overthinking can stifle the magic that comes with uncertainty.

Here are a few basic guidelines and suggestions to get you started. Remember, scrap theory is art, and art is about creating what you love and find beautiful. Having a basic understanding of how colors interact will help you achieve a harmonious balance in your color pairings, so let's start by looking at color conceptually.

COLOR TERMS TO KNOW

HUE
The pure color

VALUE
The lightness or darkness of a color

INTENSITY
The brightness of a color

TINT
A hue or color with white added

SHADE
A hue or color with black added

TONE
A hue or color with gray added

PROPORTIONALITY
How much of each color is used

COLOR CHART

Brights
Colors that are bold, saturated, and bright.

Neutrals
Grounding colors like black, gray, brown, beige, white, and denim.

Shades and Tones
Colors that have either black or gray added and are toned down. Most colors in fashion will be in this group.

COLOR STRATEGIES

ANALOGOUS

An analogous palette uses colors that sit next to each other on the color wheel. These colors naturally blend together, creating a soft, harmonious look that feels cohesive and is easy on the eyes.

COMPLEMENTARY

Complementary colors sit opposite each other on the color wheel. This bold pairing creates strong contrast and energy, making the combination vibrant and eye-catching.

MONOCHROMATIC

A monochromatic palette sticks to one base color, using its tints and shades to build depth. This creates a clean, calm look that feels intentional and effortlessly stylish.

Feel free to mix and match these strategies. Patchwork is equal parts play and personal storytelling and there's no wrong way to do it. As long as you love it, it's perfect!

HOW TO USE SCRAP THEORY TO MAKE A GARMENT

1. Choose your main fabric
This will be your anchor fabric. All the other fabrics you choose should complement this anchor fabric.

2. Pick a color strategy
Select one of the color strategies (see page 13) and pull fabrics that complement your anchor fabric. Feel free to use as many or as few fabrics as you'd like.

3. Play with shades and tones
Experiment with different shades and tones of your chosen colors to add depth and variation.

4. Add a pop
Try adding one color from the brights (see page 12) for an eye-catching pop of color.

5. Balance with neutrals
Incorporate neutral colors like black, white, gray, brown, and/or denim to ground your garment and provide versatility. Consider how a white T-shirt, black pants, or tan trench coat can balance an outfit.

THINGS TO REMEMBER WHEN BUILDING A PALETTE

Fabric with prints and pattern
Don't be afraid of prints! While prints typically have two or more colors, there's usually a dominant color you can identify. Think of that color as your base color. The other colors will act as accents that should complement your chosen color concept strategy. Prints and patterns will add visual interest and variety to your project.

Scale
Scale can add a captivating dimension to your sewing projects. Consider incorporating elements like small dots, large dots, thin stripes, thick stripes, delicate florals, or all-over floral patterns. The key is variety! Try pairing something small with something big. Working with scale adds depth and complexity, preventing a monotonous look. Remember, opposites attract!

Value variation
Combining light, medium, and dark helps to achieve depth, visual interest, and emotion.

IT'S TIME TO START ARRANGING YOUR FABRICS!

Begin by laying out your fabrics in the order you envision them appearing in your garment. To achieve balance in your color placement, ensure that your values are varied throughout your piece. For instance, avoid placing all dark colors in one concentrated area; instead, distribute them evenly. At this stage, you might find that you need to adjust your palette by adding or subtracting fabrics. Experiment to see what works best. Remember that you're aiming for overall balance.

If you're struggling to decide between a few options, take pictures so you can step back and compare them later. There are no wrong combinations, only different ones.

Sorting or storing your scraps by color helps to keep you organized!

WAYS TO APPLY SCRAP THEORY TO YOUR WARDROBE

Use pattern pieces as a guide
We design patterns with simple shapes at the top of our mind. This makes them a great jumping-off point for using up scraps. Simply apply your chosen scrap palette to any pattern and use a different type of fabric for each pattern piece.

Make fabric from scraps
Get truly creative by making a large piece of fabric from smaller scraps (see page 16). This technique has a lot of impact in a pattern with a large surface area, like a full skirt, the back of a jacket, or pant legs.

HOW TO MAKE FABRIC FROM SCRAPS

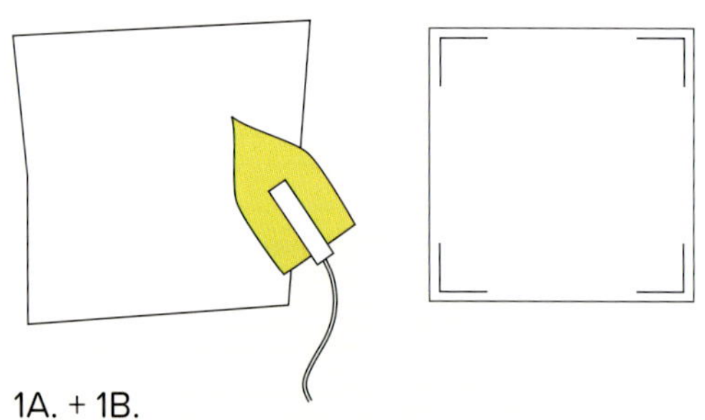

1A. + 1B.

1. Prepare scraps

A. Gently press your fabric with an iron, being careful not to stretch or distort the fabric. Do this for all your scrap fabric pieces.

B. Trim fabric so that all four corners are square. Try to maintain a straight grain. If your pieces are slightly cut on the bias, they will have a tendency to twist.

2A.

2. Join scraps

A. With right sides together, align two raw edges. Pin in place. Sew with a ½-inch (1.3cm) seam allowance. Finish seam with a zigzag stitch or serger. Press seam toward one side. Trim so that all four corners are square.

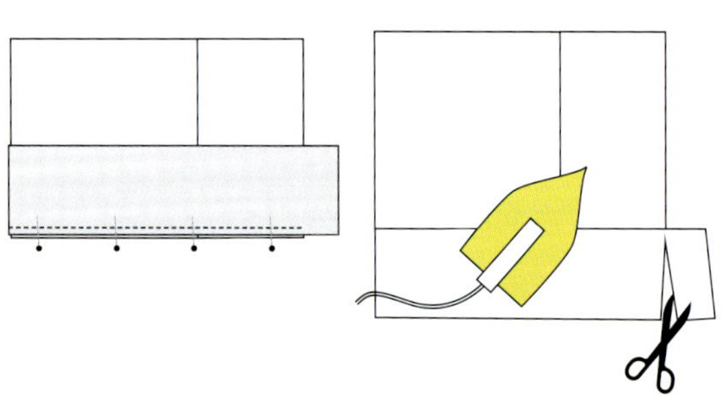

2B.

B. Continue building your fabric with remaining scrap pieces using this method until you reach the desired measurement. Once you have reached your desired measurement, you can cut your pattern piece from this new piece of fabric.

RECOMMENDED SEWING TOOLS

Sewing does not have to be complicated. Whether you're just starting out with garment sewing or quilting, these basic tools are all you need.

Sewing machine

If you're new to sewing and searching for your first machine, don't overthink it! Most sewing machines share the same basic functions; you'll need these three essential features: a straight stitch, a zigzag stitch, and a buttonhole maker.

Manual machines use dials and levers for adjustments. Electronic ones have buttons and often offer more features and stitch options. While those extras might be interesting to explore as you gain experience, they're not necessary when you're just starting out.

Our Suggestion: The Singer Heavy Duty

This model provides all the essentials in an easy-to-use format, making it perfect for honing your new sewing skills.

Serger

This machine uses multiple threads to finish raw edges and prevents the fabric from fraying. It gives that professional look on the inside of your garments. This is a machine we wanted to introduce but it is certainly not necessary for a beginner sewist. We recommend starting with a zigzag stitch on your regular sewing machine to finish raw edges. As your sewing skills and confidence grow, you may want to consider adding this machine to your sewing room.

Our Suggestion: Brother Serger, 1034D

This model offers a balance of durability, affordability, and essential features, making it perfect for a wide range of projects.

1 OF A KIND
ARTEZA
PATENTED DESIGN
OLFA

Cutting mat

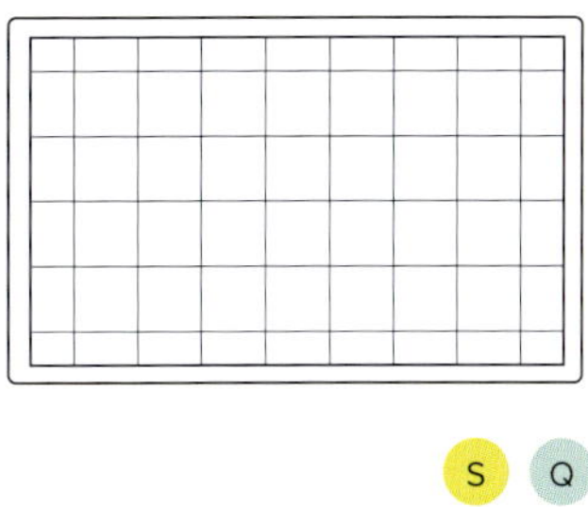

S Q

Protects your work surface while cutting.

Rotary cutter

S Q

Circular blade to help cut straight lines.

Quilt ruler

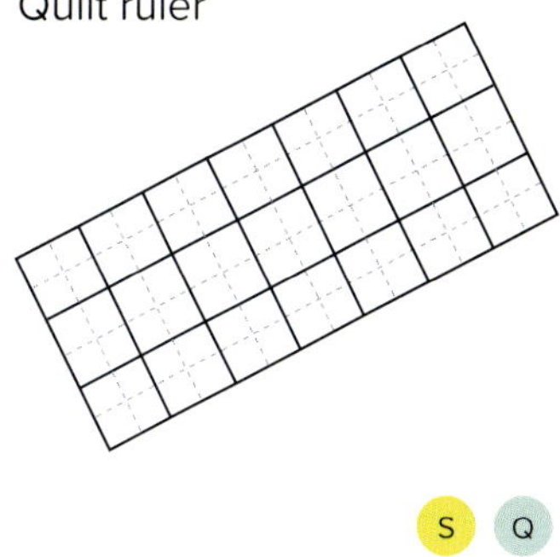

S Q

Measure and cut fabric pieces accurately.

Hera marker

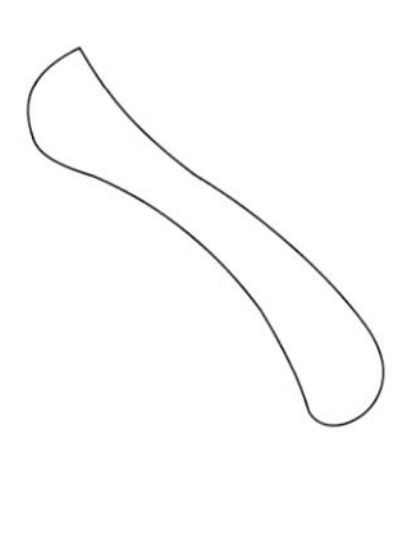

Q

Makes temporary creases in fabric.

Scissors

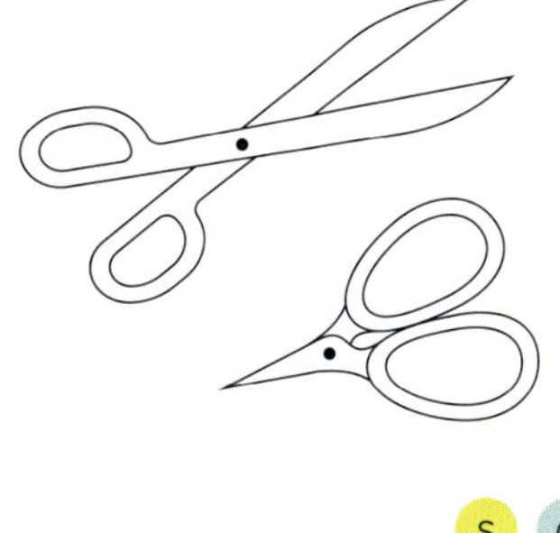

S Q

8–10-inch (20–25cm) blade for cutting fabric; small and sharp for trimming threads.

Seam ripper

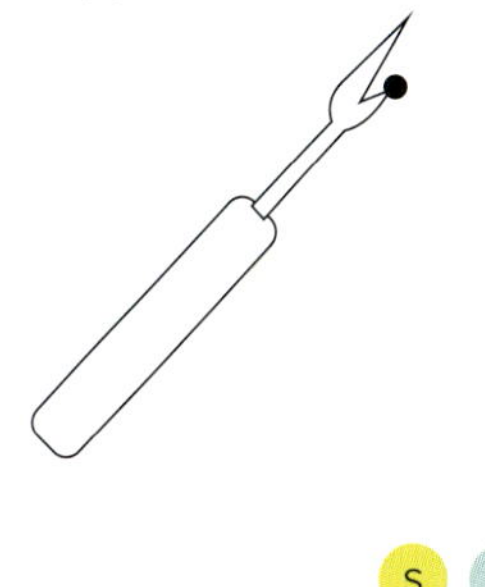

S Q

Removes stitches and seams.

Walking foot

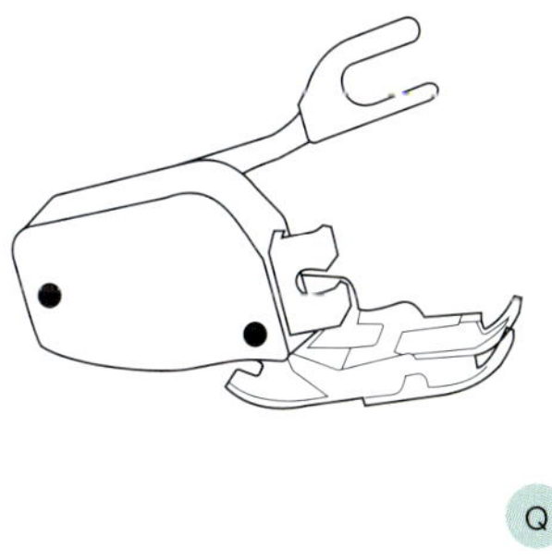

Q

Sewing machine attachment that helps feed several layers of fabric evenly.

Iron

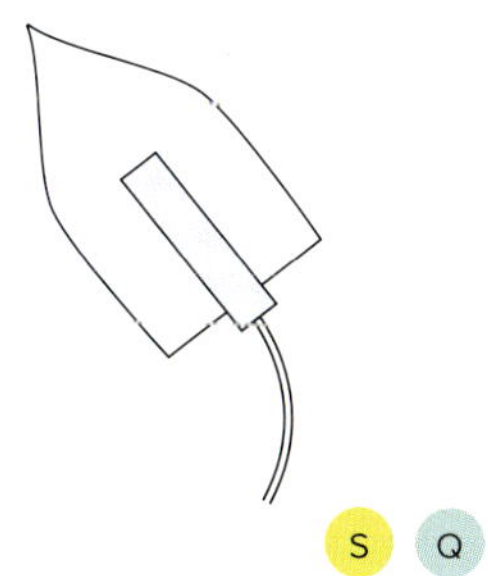

S Q

Used for pressing fabric.

Pins or clips, and weights

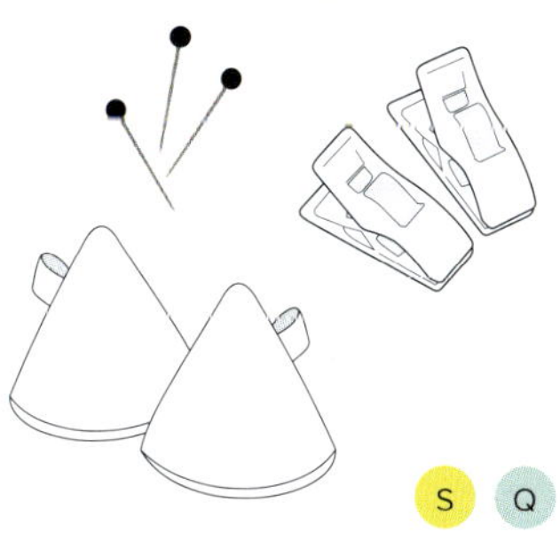

S Q

Holds multiple layers of fabric in place. Weights hold pattern pieces down on the fabric.

S Sewing  Q Quilting

FINDING YOUR FIT

To find your Matchy Matchy size, start by taking your body measurements at these three major levels, then compare your measurements to our body measurement size chart below. The chart measurements are given in inches, then centimeters.

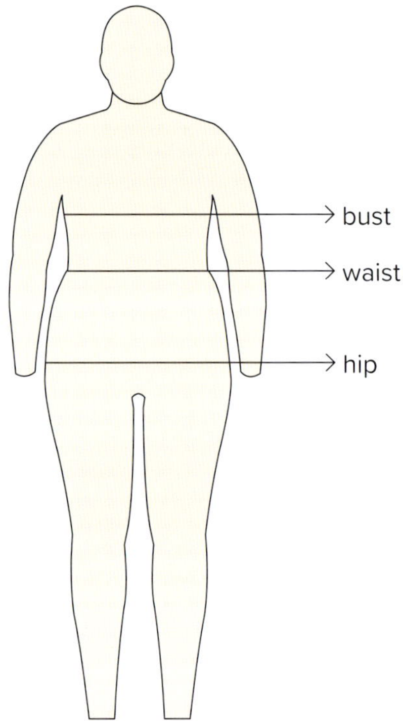

Our sewing patterns are drafted for a 5ft 5in (165cm) individual.

Bust
Represents the fullest point on chest.

How to measure
Wrap measuring tape around the back, under the arms, and across the fullest part of the bust.

bust .... *date* ....

Waist
Represents the narrowest part of your torso, typically just above the belly button.

How to measure
Wrap measuring tape around the waist comfortably.

waist .... *date* ....

Hip
Represents the fullest point below the waist.

How to measure
Wrap measuring tape around the hip comfortably.

hip .... *date* ....

	XXS	XS	S	M	L	XL	2XL	3XL	4XL	5XL	6XL
Chest	31–32 (79–81)	33–34 (84–86.5)	35–36 (89–91.5)	37–38 (94–96.5)	39½–41 (101–104)	42½–44 (108–112)	46–48 (117–122)	50–52 (127–132)	54–56 (137–142)	58–60 (147–152)	62–64 (157–163)
Waist	24–25 (61–63.5)	26–27 (66–68.5)	28–29 (71–74)	30–31 (76–79)	32½–34 (83–86.5)	35½–37 (90–94)	39–41 (99–104)	43–45 (109–114)	47–49 (119.5–124)	51–53 (130–135)	55–57 (140–145)
Hip	34–35 (86.5–89)	36–37 (91.5–94)	38–39 (96.5–99)	40–41 (101.5–104)	42½–44 (108–112)	45½–47 (116–119.5)	49–51 (124.5–130)	53–55 (135–140)	57–59 (145–150)	61–63 (155–160)	65–67 (165–170)

Your Matchy Matchy size .... *date* ....

Understanding ease

Ease is the amount of extra room between your body measurements and the finished garment measurements.

Why is ease important?

We need ease to allow for movement. The amount of ease represented in a garment can also reflect intended style and shape. To figure out how much ease a pattern has, simply subtract your body measurement from the finished garment measurements listed on the pattern. This difference is the amount of ease built into the garment.

Finding your perfect fit

At Matchy Matchy, we believe that fit is all about comfort and personal preference. Our patterns are intentionally designed with a cool and casual vibe—think easy-going, comfortable styles with a little extra room to move. That's why we include about 4–6 inches (10–15cm) of built-in ease in most of our designs. If this feels like your ideal fit, the size you find using the body measurement size chart will likely align perfectly with the finished garment size chart.

Remember, the best size for you is the one that feels right for your body and your style. Just because you measure a size medium on the body measurement size chart, doesn't mean you have to stick with that size. You're in control of your fit!

Here's how you can adjust:

- If you love a relaxed, oversized look, size up for more ease and a looser fit.
- If you prefer a more tailored, form-fitting look, sizing down will give you a closer fit with less ease.
- For garments without closures (like zippers or buttons), make sure there's enough ease to get the garment on and off easily!

We encourage you to experiment with different sizes to find what makes you feel your best. Each pattern can be adjusted to match your personal style, and that's part of the fun! Remember, sewing is all about making something that's uniquely yours. So, take the time to find your ideal fit—whether it's relaxed and roomy or sleek and fitted, the choice is yours!

ACCESSING AND USING THE PATTERNS

Great news! All of our sewing patterns are available as easy-to-use PDF downloads, so you can get started on your sewing journey in no time. Each pattern can be accessed by scanning the QR code below—super simple! Once you scan the QR code, you'll have two options for downloading your pattern.

Print-at-home file
This file contains all the pattern pieces spread across several pages, which you'll print on your home printer. After printing, you'll tile the pages together (think of it like a puzzle!) and tape them to create the full-sized pattern. It's a great option if you want to get started right away and don't mind spending a little time piecing it together.

A0 copy shop file
If you'd prefer to skip the printing and taping, this file is for you! The A0 file is a full-sized version of the pattern, ready to be printed at your local copy shop. Just upload the file to your favorite print shop and they'll print the entire pattern on a large sheet of paper, saving you time and effort.

Once you've downloaded your file and have your pattern ready, you're all set to get started on your sewing project. Remember, both options give you the same pattern pieces—you just choose the method that works best for you. Whether you're a print-at-home pro or you prefer the ease of getting it printed at a copy shop, you'll have the perfect pattern ready to go!

Scan to access the patterns

ASSEMBLING YOUR PRINT-AT-HOME PATTERN

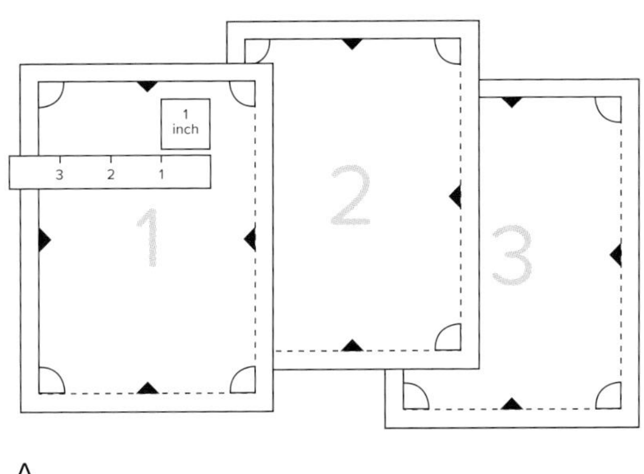

A.

A. Make sure that your printer scaling is turned off and is set to print at 100%. Print page 1 first and measure to make sure the 1-inch (2.5cm) square is the correct size.

B.

B. Print all the pages. Refer to the assembly guide located on the printed pattern and cut off any borders that will align with the next piece.

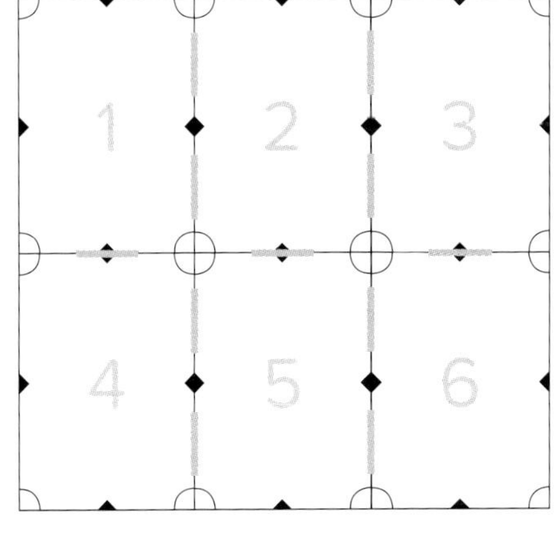

C.

C. Tape pages together from left to right, matching the circles and letters. The thin border lines on each page should butt up against each other, not overlap. Tape the rows together to complete the pattern.

PATTERN TERMS, SYMBOLS, AND MEANING

Sewing patterns can seem a bit intimidating at first, but don't worry! Once you learn a few key symbols and their meanings, you'll be sewing with confidence in no time.

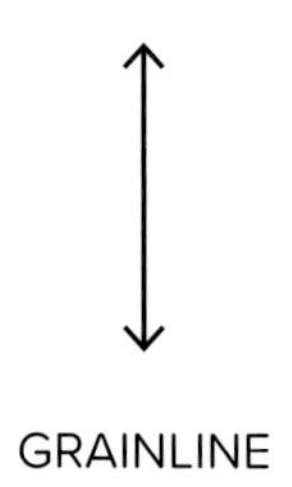

GRAINLINE

The grainline is the direction that fibers are woven in your fabric. A grainline arrow will be indicated on each pattern piece telling you what direction your pattern pieces should be placed on your fabric. Following the grainline is how your final garments hang nicely on your body.

How to use grainline arrows when cutting pattern pieces

- Identify the grainline: The grainline runs parallel to the selvage edge. The selvage edge is the tightly woven edge found along both lengthwise sides of your fabric.
- Align with selvage: Place your pattern piece on your fabric so that the grainline arrow is parallel to the selvage.

⊥

NOTCH

⊥⊥

DOUBLE NOTCH

Notches serve as alignment guides, ensuring that two pattern pieces are joined correctly. By indicating key meeting points, notches help you achieve a smoothly fitting garment.

How to use notches when cutting pattern pieces

- Transfer notches to fabric: Make a small cut into your fabric every time you see a notch appear on your sewing pattern. Notches should be cut smaller than the pattern's seam allowance, typically notches should not exceed ¼ inch (0.6cm). This way it will not be visible on your final garment.
- Single notch: Represents the front of garment.
- Double notch: Represents the back of garment.

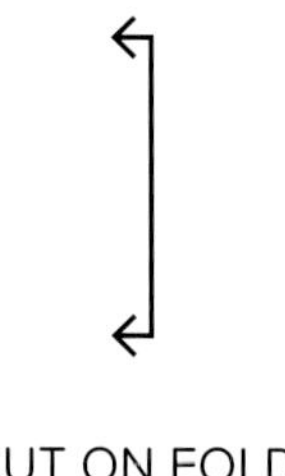

CUT ON FOLD

This symbol means that the pattern piece represents only half of the intended shape. You will need to cut this piece on the fold of your fabric.

How to use "cut on fold" when cutting pattern pieces

- Place the edge of the pattern piece against the fold line of your fabric.
- Pin pattern piece to fabric.
- Cut your fabric without cutting through the fold.

USING YOUR PATTERN

Trace or cut out your desired size from the paper pattern.

Determine how much fabric you will need by finding your size and the width of your fabric on the fabric requirements chart. Fabric is typically sold in 44-inch (112cm) or 54-inch (137cm) widths. Both of these are listed for all our patterns.

If you're using new fabric, be sure to prewash it as you would wash your final garment. If your fabric is patchworked from existing pieces, it's already been washed and can be used as is.

Prepare your fabric by folding it in half, selvage to selvage. Folding your fabric in half before cutting will yield two opposite pieces with just one cut. Check the cutting layout, because some pieces may need to be cut from a single layer. You can download cutting layouts for each pattern by following the QR code on page 22.

Lay your paper pattern pieces on top of the fabric, making sure the grainline marked on each piece runs parallel with the selvage of the fabric. Secure in place with pins or pattern weights. Cut fabric around the pattern pieces.

For pattern pieces marked "cut on fold," align the pattern with the folded edge of the fabric, right at the fold arrow. Cut around the pattern piece without cutting through the fold; this will give you one full piece.

GARMENT CONSTRUCTION ANATOMY

neckline
shoulder seam
armhole
armscye
side seam
hem

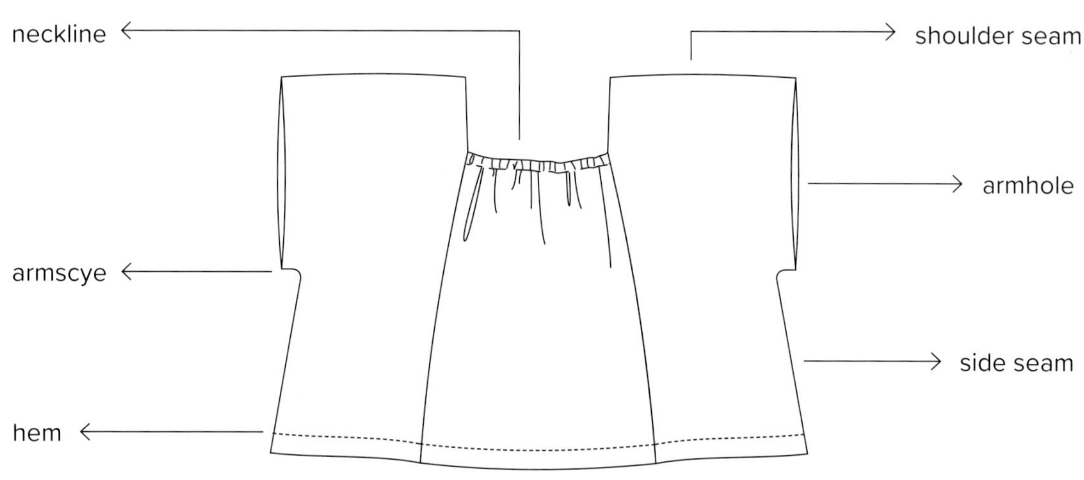

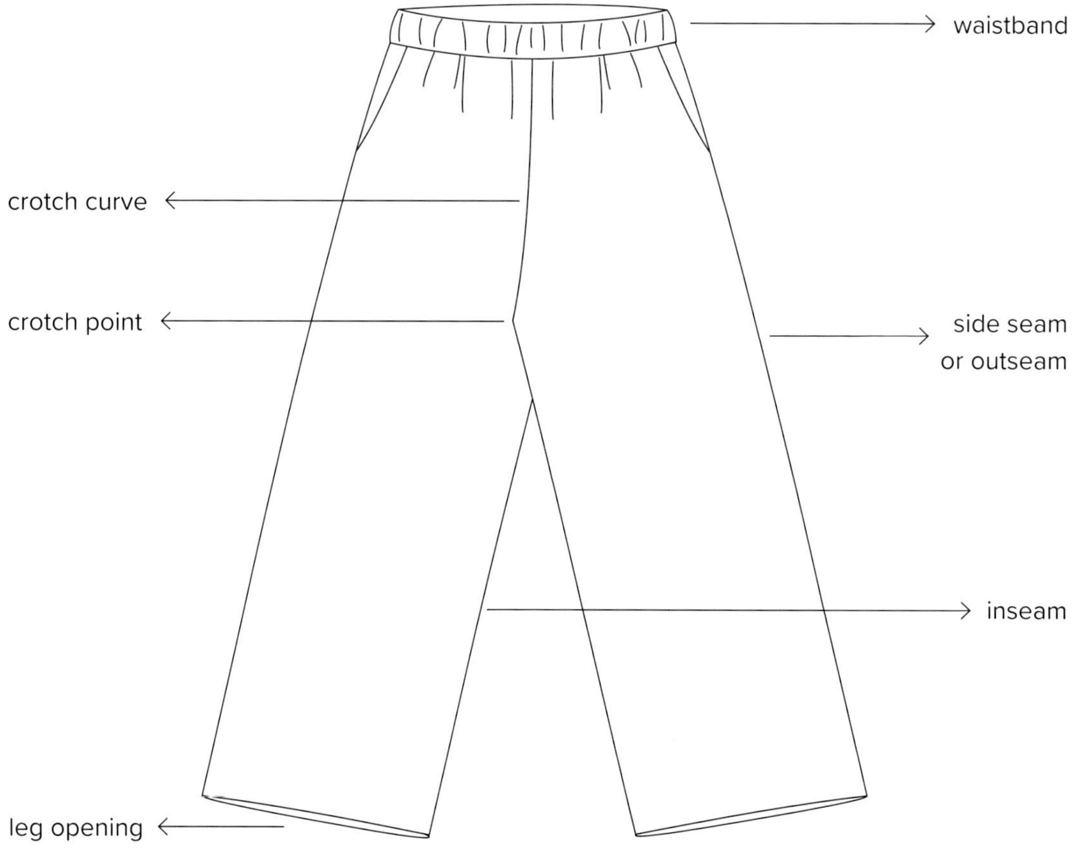

waistband
crotch curve
crotch point
side seam
or outseam
inseam
leg opening

FREQUENTLY USED TERMS

To help you navigate our sewing directions with ease, we've put together a quick reference sheet of basic sewing terms that you'll encounter frequently. Please keep this handy for future reference.

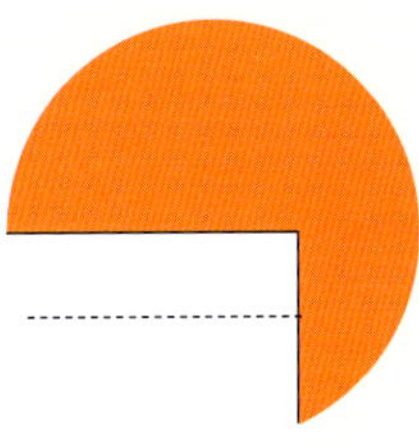

Straight stitch
The straight stitch is the foundation stitch used to connect two pieces of fabric. It's typically the default stitch on your sewing machine. The stitch length determines the size of each stitch. For most woven fabrics, a stitch length between 2 and 3 is recommended.

Raw edge
The raw edge is the cut edge of your fabric.

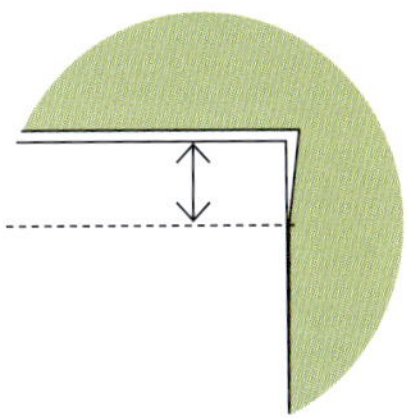

Seam allowance
The seam allowance is the extra fabric between the stitch line and the raw edge. The distance of the seam allowance will vary from seam to seam so always refer back to the pattern instructions for recommended seam allowance.

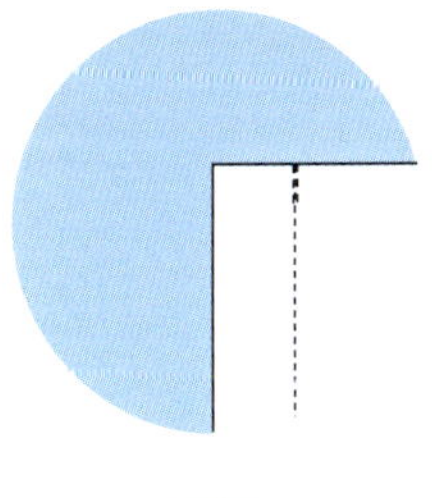

Backstitch
A backstitch secures the sewn stitches and prevents stitches from unraveling. To backstitch, sew in reverse 3–5 stitches over your existing stitch line at the beginning and end of the seam.

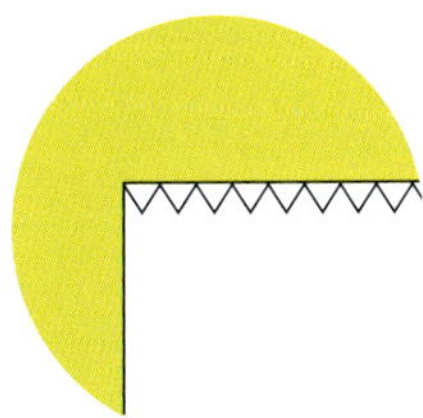

Zigzag stitch
A zigzag stitch is simply a stitch line formed in a zigzag shape. This stitch is often used as a finishing stitch on the raw edge of fabric. A finishing stitch will help prevent cut edges from fraying during wash and wear.

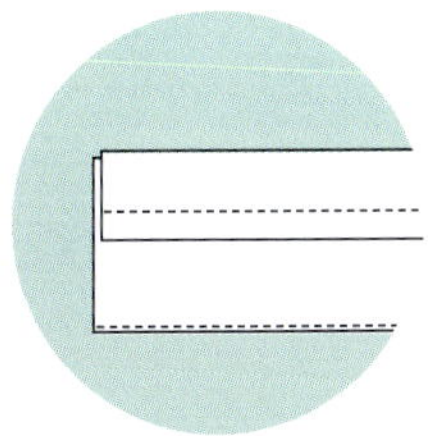

Top stitch and edge stitch
The terms top stitch and edge stitch can be used interchangeably. However, a general difference is a top stitch is usually decorative and sewn ¼–½ inch (0.6–1.3cm) away from the seam. An edge stitch is a stitch sewn very close to the edge, usually 1⁄16–⅛ inch (0.2–0.3cm) away from the seam.

TECHNIQUES: YOUR SEWING TOOLKIT

Welcome to the techniques section! Think of this as your sewing toolkit—inside you'll find the essential skills that will help you bring your sewing projects to life. These techniques aren't just useful for the patterns in this book; they're the same techniques you'll encounter in almost every sewing project, from beginner projects to more advanced makes.

Learning these skills will give you the confidence to tackle patterns with ease, and the best part—they get easier with practice! Whether it's stitching a neat hem, inserting a pocket, or experimenting with quilting, mastering these techniques is the key to making your sewing journey more enjoyable.

As you move through the book, you'll see these techniques pop up again and again. Each time you use them, you'll be building your sewing knowledge and improving your skills—one stitch at a time. So take your time, practice, and most importantly, have fun with it.

You've got this!

Bias binding is simply a way to finish raw edges when sewing garments.

BIAS BINDING

Bias tape is a strip of fabric cut at a 45-degree angle—this is called cutting on the bias. Cutting fabric this way gives it a bit of stretch and flexibility, which is exactly what we need when sewing around curves like necklines and armholes. When that strip is folded into quarters, it becomes bias binding.

In this book we will be using bias binding to finish all necklines and armholes. We love this method because it's neat, versatile, and depending on how you apply it, it can be a subtle finish on the inside or a design feature on the outside of your garment. It's one of those techniques that's fun to experiment with and super handy to have in your sewing toolbox. Once you get the hang of it, you'll find yourself using it everywhere—from garments to quilts to handmade accessories.

Keep fabric scraps from piling up by turning them into bias tape as you go—your future self will thank you for it!

Bias tape can be cut to the exact length you need from a single piece of fabric, or it can be pieced together to make a long, continuous strip. We'll be using the piecing method because it's efficient, uses up fabric scraps, and gives you a generous stash of bias tape for future projects.

1A.

MAKING BIAS TAPE

1. Cut fabric strips

A. Cut 1⅝-inch (4cm) wide strips on a 45-degree angle from your fabric using your quilter's ruler, rotary cutter, and cutting mat. Use fabric that is at least 10 inches (25.5cm) high by any width. The wider the fabric the more bias tape you'll get. You will not use the fabric corners as the strips will be too short and result in too many seams.

2. Connect fabric strips

A. Cut off the diagonal edges of the fabric strips.

B. With right sides together, place two of the strips at 90-degree angles and line up the edges. Sew diagonally across the corners. Repeat to join all the strips.

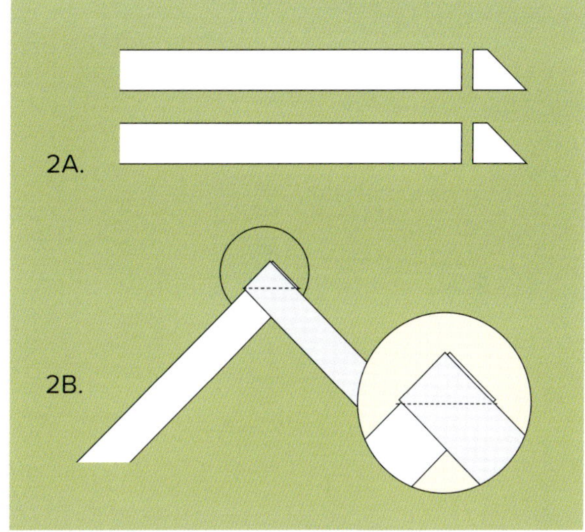

C. Trim all seams to ⅜ inch (1cm) and press them open. Your bias tape is complete! Now it's time to turn your bias tape into bias binding.

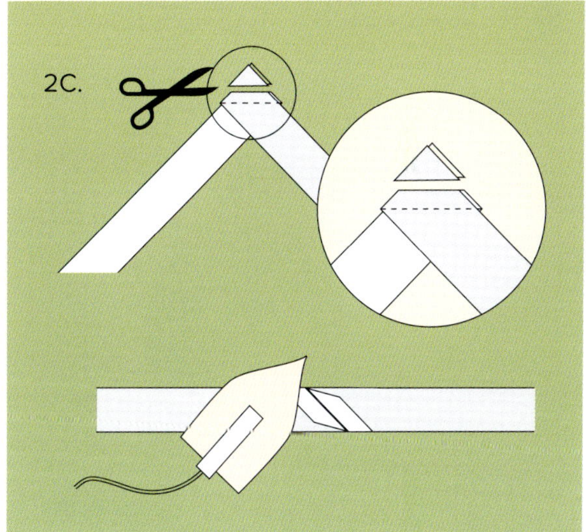

3. Make bias binding

A. With wrong sides together, fold the bias tape in half lengthwise. Press in place to form a crease. Open back up.

B. Fold top and bottom edges toward the wrong side to meet the center crease. Press in place.

C. Fold in half along center crease. Press in place.

D. Unfold when ready to use.

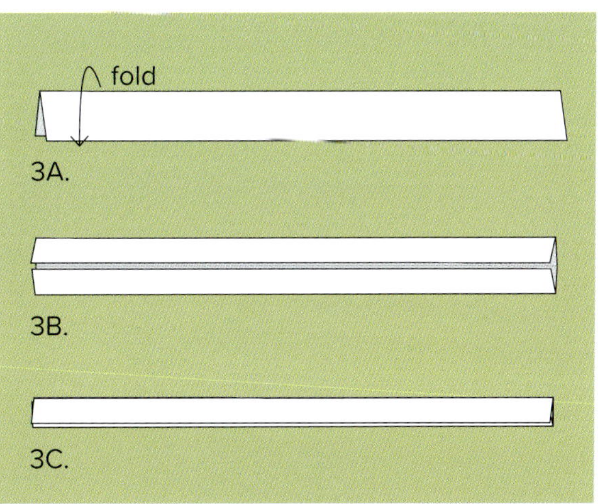

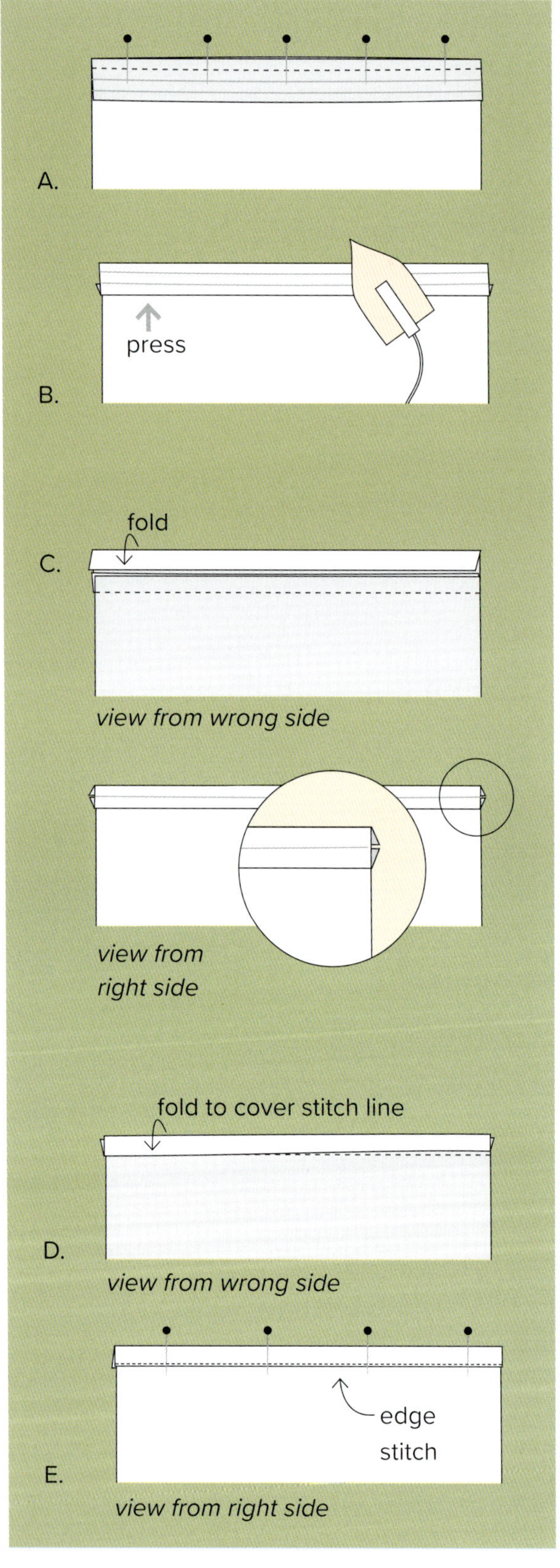

OPEN END BIAS BINDING

Use this method when the raw ends will be enclosed at a different stage.

How to attach bias binding with open ends

A. With right sides together, align bias to raw edge of garment. Without stretching the bias, pin in place. Sew with a ⅜-inch (1cm) seam allowance, using the press line closest to upper raw edge as a guide.

B. Press the bias and seam allowance up and away from the garment.

C. Using the upper press line as a guide, fold top raw edge of bias ⅜ inch (1cm) toward the wrong side. Press in place.

D. Using the center crease mark as a guide, fold bias over one more time toward wrong side, enclosing all the raw edges. Make sure folded bias extends just past the stitch line made in step A. Press and pin in place.

E. Edge stitch the bias binding with a minimal seam allowance, making sure to catch the folded bias on the back.

FINISHED END BIAS BINDING

This method is commonly used for necklines with button plackets or openings.

How to attach bias with finished ends

A. With right sides together, extend bias ½ inch (1.3cm) from starting point. Fold extension back onto the wrong side. Pin in place. Without stretching the bias, continue to pin along the opening. When you reach the end, trim bias so that it extends ½ inch (1.3cm) past the edge. Fold extension back onto the wrong side. Pin in place. Sew bias with a ⅜-inch (1cm) seam allowance.

B. Press the bias and seam allowance up and away from the garment. The bias extensions will naturally flip to form a clean edge along the short ends of the bias.

C. Using the upper press line as a guide, fold top raw edge of bias ⅜ inch (1cm) toward the wrong side. Press in place.

D. Using the center crease mark as a guide, fold bias over one more time toward wrong side, enclosing all the raw edges. Make sure folded bias extends just past the stitch line made in step A. Press and pin in place.

E. Edge stitch the bias binding with a minimal seam allowance, making sure to catch the folded bias on the back.

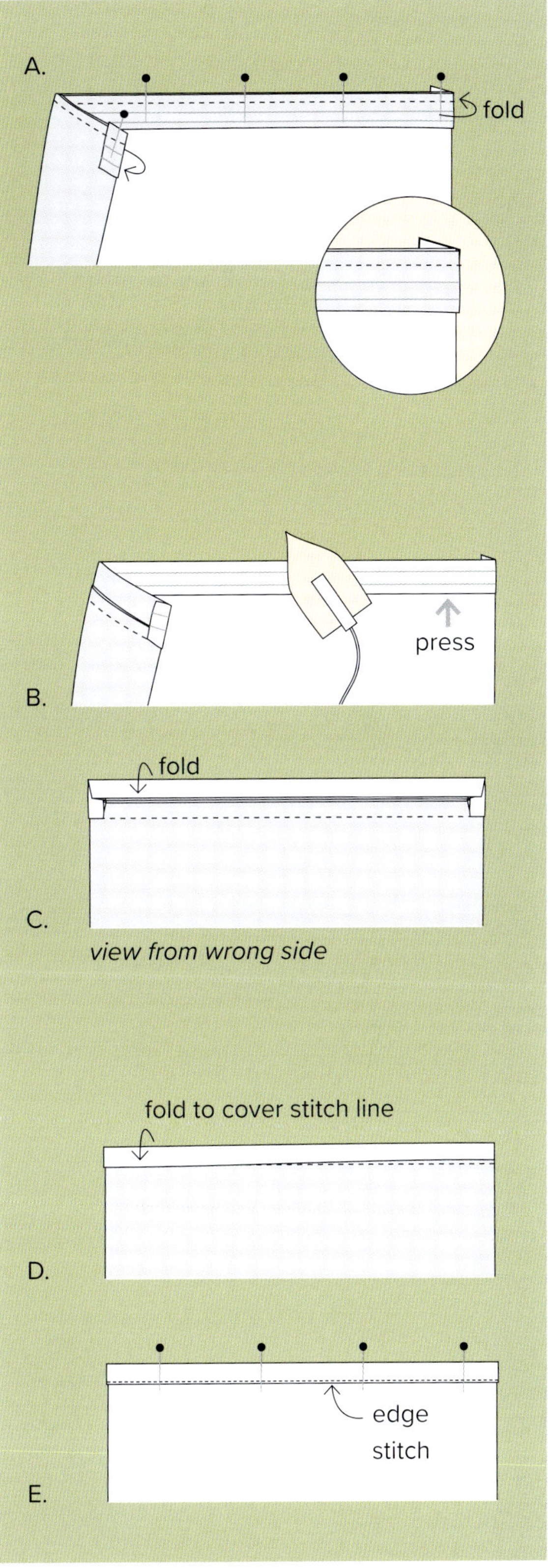

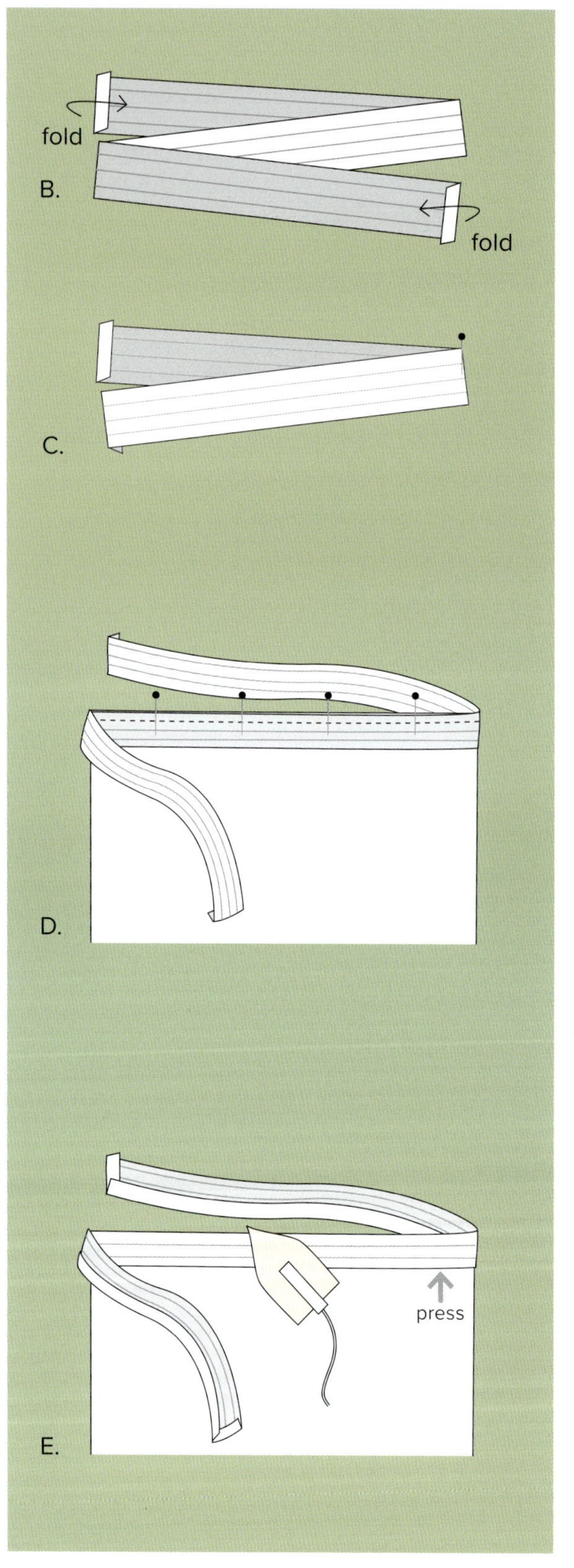

BIAS BINDING WITH TAILS

This is when the bias binding extends past the edge of your garment, creating a long tail commonly used for tie closures.

How to attach bias with tails

A. Cut bias to length needed.

B. Open out and fold both short ends ⅜ inch (1cm) toward the wrong side. Press in place.

C. Find center point by folding bias in half lengthwise. Mark center with a pin or very small notch.

D. Right sides together, align bias to raw edge of garment, matching center point of bias to center point of garment. Pin outward from center point in both directions without stretching the bias. Long tails will extend out on either side which will later become ties. Sew with a ⅜-inch (1cm) seam allowance using the press line closest to upper raw edge as a guide. Start and stop where bias and garment meet.

E. Press bias and seam allowance up and away from garment. Using that same press line as a guide continue pressing down the tails, making sure each end is still folder over.

F. Using the upper press line as a guide, fold top raw edge of bias 3⁄8 inch (1cm) toward the wrong side. Continue down the tails. Press in place.

G. Using the center crease mark as a guide, fold bias over one more time toward wrong side, enclosing all the raw edges. Make sure folded bias extends just past the stitch line made in step A. Press and pin in place.

H. Working from the right side of the garment, edge stitch bias binding with a minimal seam allowance, starting from one end of tail and working around the garment to the other end of tail. When going around the garment, make sure to catch the folded edge of the bias that is on the wrong side of garment.

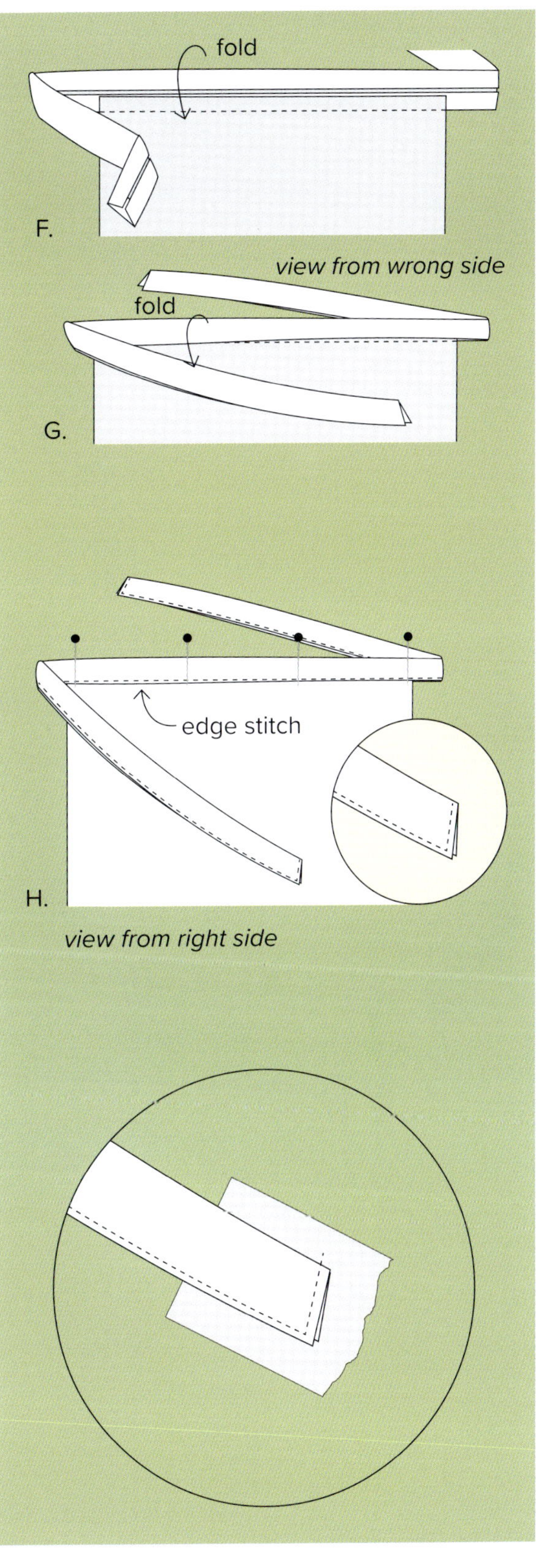

Quick tip: *The ends of the tails can be tricky to sew. Put a small piece of paper under them, then sew the tail directly on top of the paper. This will keep the skinny tail ends stable while sewing. Carefully pull away the paper when complete.*

CLOSED LOOP BIAS BINDING

This method is used for circular binding such as neck openings and armholes.

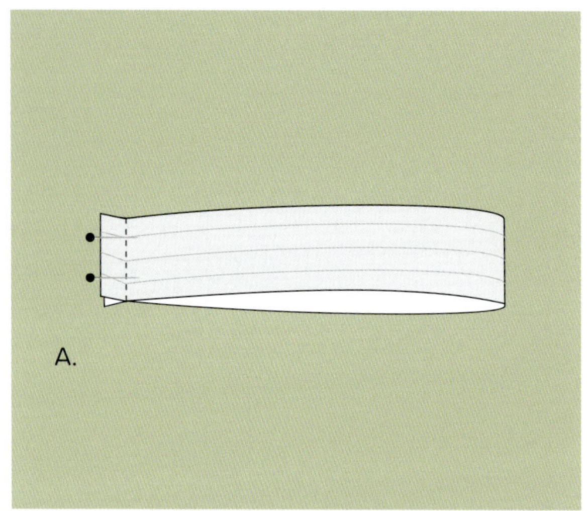

How to attach closed loop bias binding

A. With right sides together, pin short ends of bias and sew with a ½-inch (1.3cm) seam allowance, creating a loop. Press seam open. If making an armband, this is a good time to make sure the armband is a good fit. Slide your arm through the loop and see if you like where the armband lands. Adjust armband length as needed.

B.

view from right side

B. With right sides together, align bias to armscye, matching bias seam to underarm seam. Pin in place without stretching the bias. Sew bias to armscye with a ⅜-inch (1cm) seam allowance, using the press line closest to the armscye as a guide. Start and stop where bias and armscye meet.

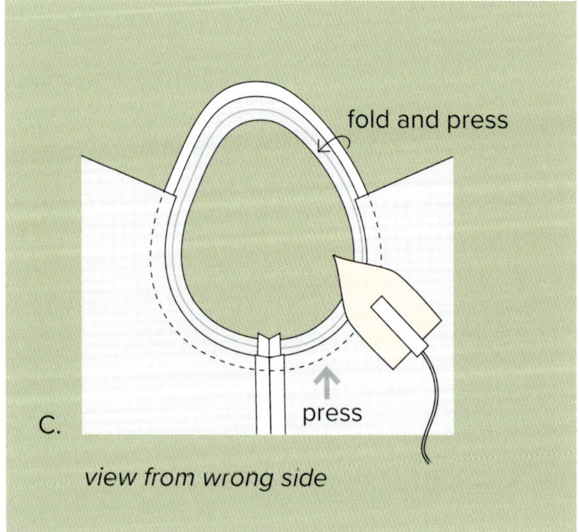

view from wrong side

C. Press bias and seam allowance up and away from garment. Using that same press line as a guide, continue pressing around the bias loop.

Quick tip: *Illustrations show closed loop bias binding that creates an arm strap. The same basic principles apply when doing a neck opening or regular armholes.*

D. Using the inner press line as a guide, fold inner raw edge of bias loop ⅜ inch (1cm) toward the wrong side. Continue around entire bias loop. Press in place.

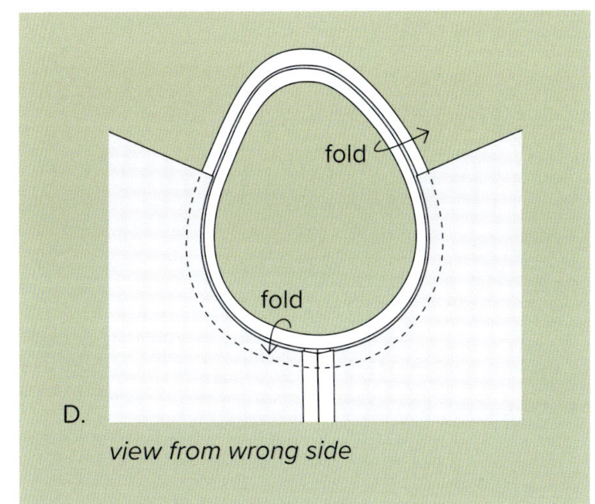

view from wrong side

E. Using the center crease mark as a guide, fold bias over one more time toward wrong side, enclosing all the raw edges. Continue around the entire loop, making sure the folded bias extends just past the stitch line made in step A. Press and pin in place.

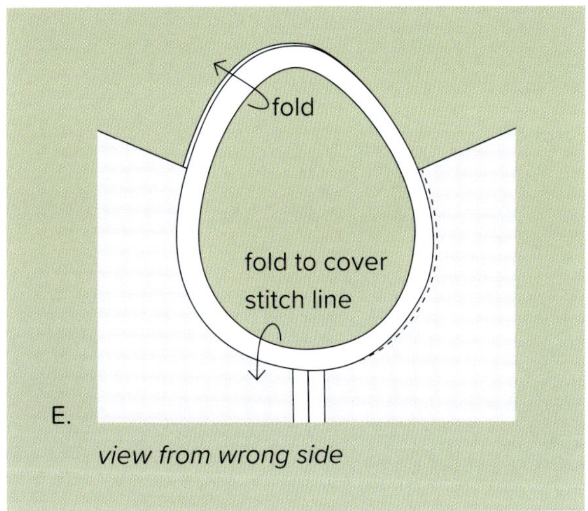

view from wrong side

F. Working from the right side of the garment, edge stitch bias binding with a minimal seam allowance around entire loop. When sewing around the loop, make sure to catch the folded edge of the bias that is on the other side.

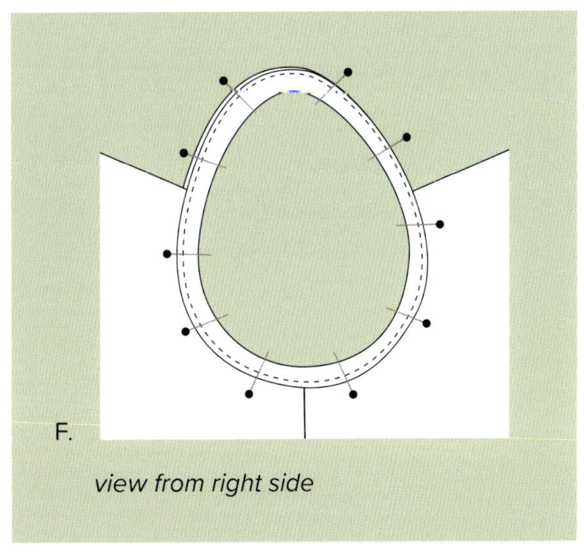

view from right side

Staystitch immediately after cutting your fabric to keep curved edges from stretching.

STAYSTITCHING

Staystitching is simply a long straight stitch sewn on fabric that is cut on a curve or on an angle. Because curves and diagonals are cut across the bias, staystitching will help to prevent stretching or warping during sewing. It is most often seen on necklines, armholes, facings, and collars.

If you want a nice-fitting garment, don't skip the staystitching.

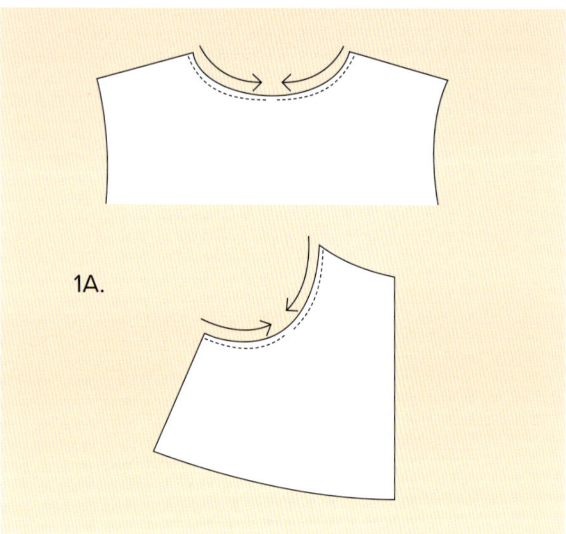

1. How to staystitch around a curve

A. Sew a straight stitch ⅛–¼ inch (0.3–0.6cm) away from the curved edge. Start from one side and sew toward the center. Cut thread. Then start from the other side and sew to meet back at center. Cut thread. Staystitching from each outer end toward the center will help keep the fabric from stretching.

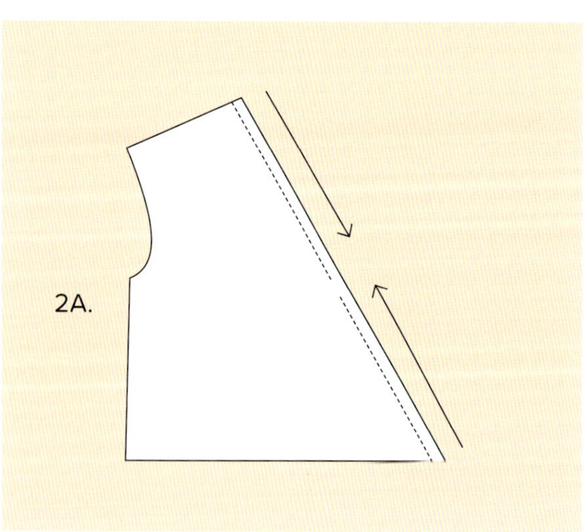

2. How to staystitch on a diagonal

A. Sew a straight stitch ⅛–¼ inch (0.3–0.6cm) along the edge of your bias cut fabric. Start from one side and sew toward the center. Cut thread. Then start from the other side and sew to meet back at center. Cut thread. Staystitching from each outer end toward the center will help keep the fabric from stretching.

GATHERING

This method can be used when making skirts and dresses, puffy sleeves, and voluminous necklines. You can also use gathering to create a ruffled edge that can be attached to another piece of fabric.

Gathering creates volume and fullness in your garments.

How to create gathers

A. Sew two rows of basting stitches along the top raw edge. Sew first row at ¼ inch (0.6cm) and second row at ⅝ inch (1.5cm), using the longest stitch length on your machine. Leave a thread tail of 3 inches (8cm) at beginning and end of stitches. Do not backstitch on either end.

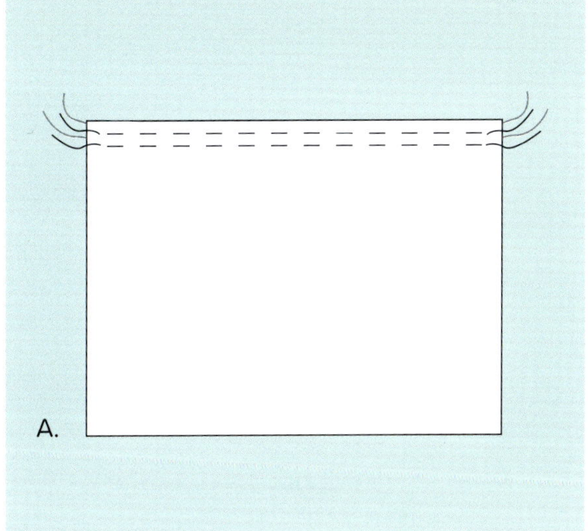

B. From the wrong side, gently pull the bobbin thread tails from one end and push the fabric along the threads toward center notch. Repeat the same process for other end. Evenly distribute gathers to desired length.

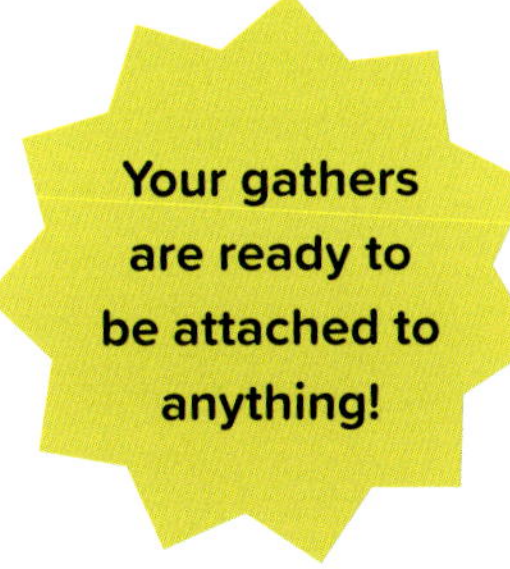

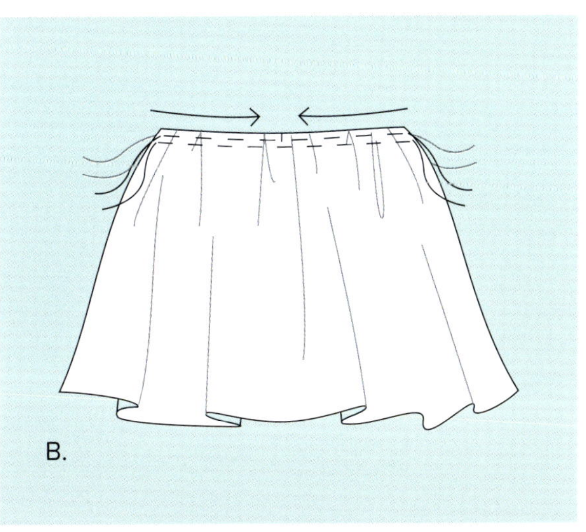

Hemming is a way to finish a raw edge around the border of a garment.

HEMMING

Hemming is a finishing method where a raw edge is folded, then sewn. You often see this on the bottom edge of pants, skirts, dresses, shirts, and sleeves. In this book we will be using the double-fold hem technique. A double-fold hem is when the raw edge of the fabric is folded over twice, then sewn. The hem allowance is the amount the hem is folded. The hem allowance will be determined within each pattern.

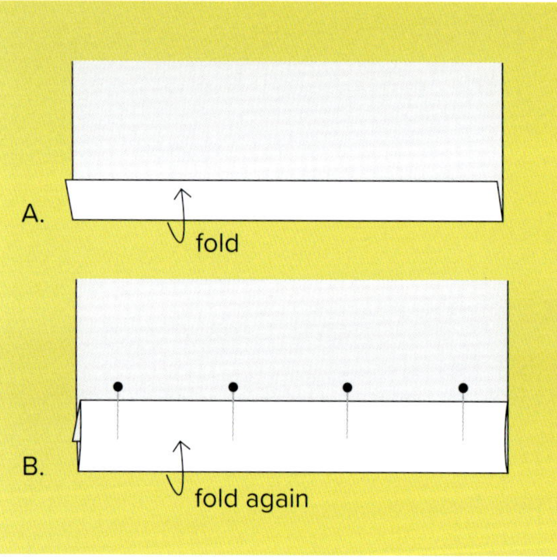

How to sew a double-fold hem

A. Fold hem toward wrong side by the amount indicated on your pattern. Press in place, making sure the hemline is straight.

B. Fold hem again toward wrong side by the amount indicated on your pattern. Press in place, making sure the hemline is straight. Pin in place.

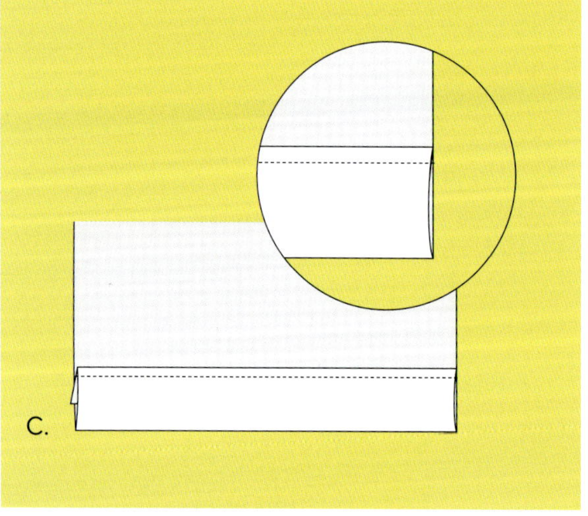

C. Sew with a ⅛-inch (0.3cm) seam allowance along the folded edge to secure hem in place.

TIES

Ties are a simple and versatile way to close a garment at the front, back, or side. They're easy to make and can be cut to any length or width, depending on the look you're going for. Narrow ties create a delicate finish, while wider ones make more of a statement. The process is beginner-friendly and fun, so engage your creativity and see what you come up with!

Ties are a cute and customizable way to close your garment.

How to make ties

A. To form a crease, fold tie in half lengthwise so that wrong sides are touching. Press in place then open back up.

B. Fold one short end ¼ inch (0.6cm) toward wrong side. Press in place.

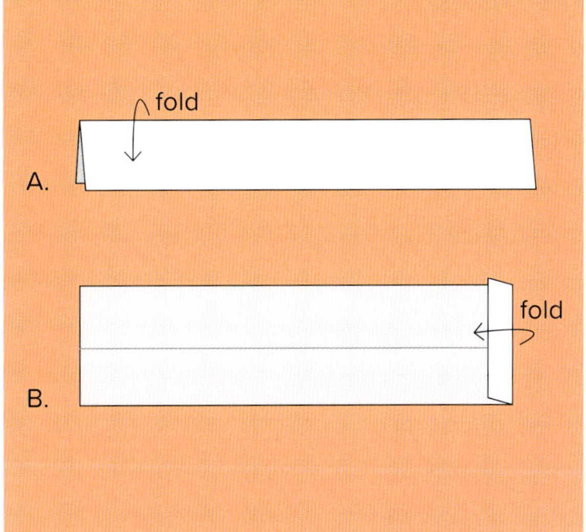

C. Fold top and bottom edges toward wrong side to meet center crease. Press in place.

D. Fold tie in half using center crease as a guide. Press in place. Edge stitch along double-folded short end and double-folded long end to close tie. Repeat for other tie.

See page 35 for tips on sewing ends of tails.

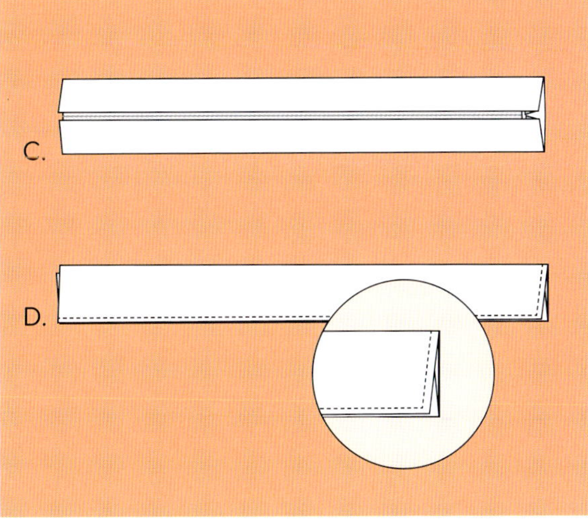

PATCH POCKET

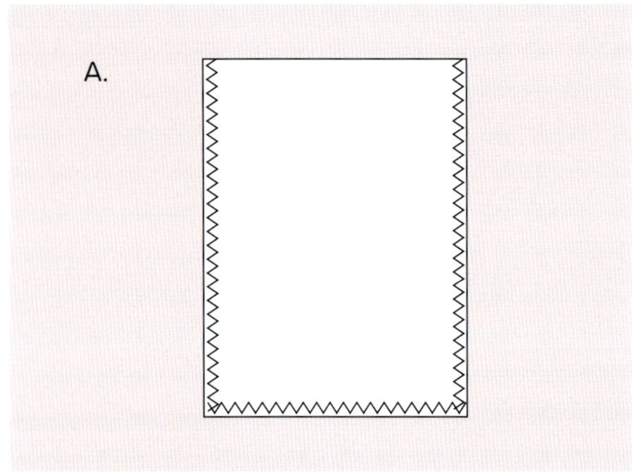

How to make a patch pocket

A. Finish the two sides and bottom edge of pocket with a zigzag stitch or serger.

Finishing stitch will not be illustrated in future steps.

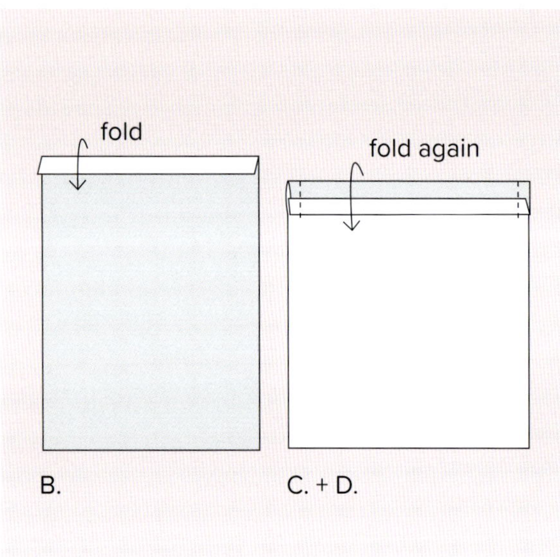

B. With wrong side facing up, fold top raw edge down by ½ inch (1.3cm) toward wrong side of fabric. Press in place.

C. With right side facing up, fold top edge down again by 1 inch (2.5cm), but this time toward the right side of the fabric.

D. Sew the outer folded edges with a ½-inch (1.3cm) seam allowance.

Fold measurements will vary depending on your pattern. Refer to your pattern for exact fold measurements.

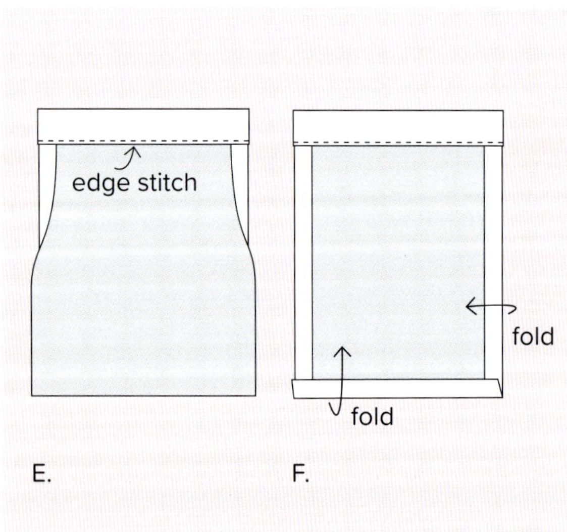

E. Flip top of pocket right side out, making sure corners are square. Press in place. Edge stitch using a ⅛-inch (0.3cm) seam allowance from bottom fold line.

F. Fold the two sides and the bottom edge by ½ inch (1.3cm) toward wrong side of the fabric.

INSEAM POCKET

How to attach inseam pockets

A. Right sides together, pin pocket to side panel, matching at notches. Sew with a ⅜-inch (1cm) seam allowance.

B. Finish seam with a zigzag stitch or serger, starting and stopping 1 inch (2.5cm) above and below the pocket opening.

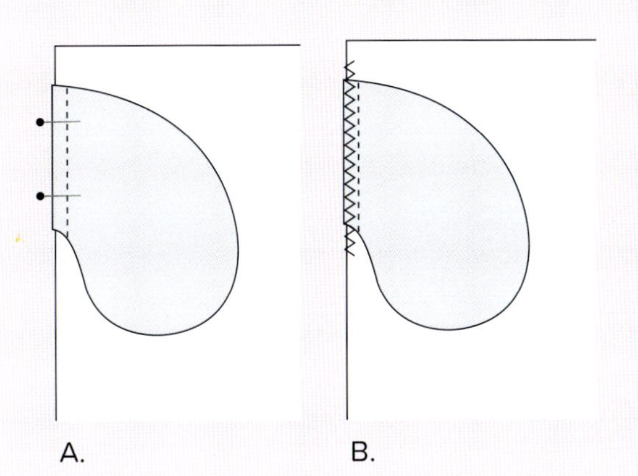

C. Press pocket and seam allowances away from the garment. Under stitch the pocket with a ⅛-inch (0.3cm) seam allowance, making sure to sew through all layers. This will ensure your pockets stay in place and not be visible from the right side of your garment.

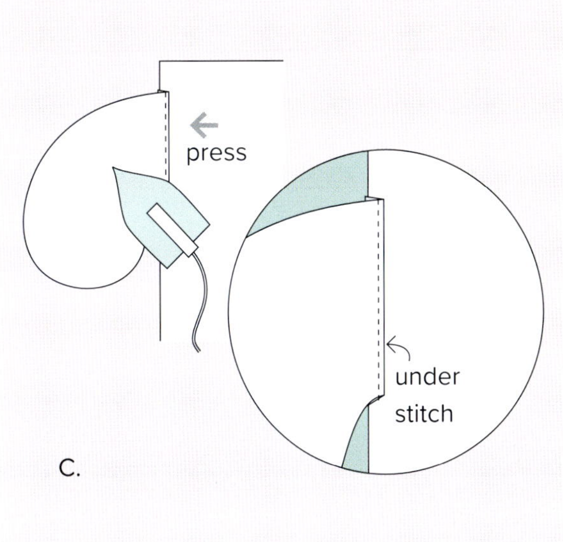

D. With right sides together, match side seams and pocket. Pin in place. Sew with a ½-inch (1.3cm) seam allowance along side seam and around pocket. Make sure to capture the under stitch line within this stitch when going around the pocket. Finish seam with a zigzag stitch or serger. Press seam toward the front to ensure your inseam pocket falls toward the front of your garment.

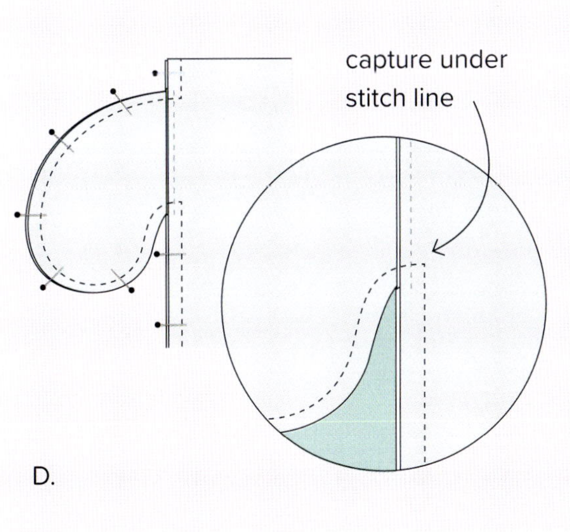

Quilting is the process of joining layers of fabric together with a stitched pattern.

QUILTING

Quilting adds texture, warmth, and a beautiful handmade feel to any garment. It's what gives a piece that cozy, lived-in comfort—like your favorite jacket or a treasured heirloom. Quilted details can be subtle or bold, and they bring a special touch that makes your project feel extra personal. For the patterns in this book we will be quilting two layers of fabric only: The main fabric and the batting.

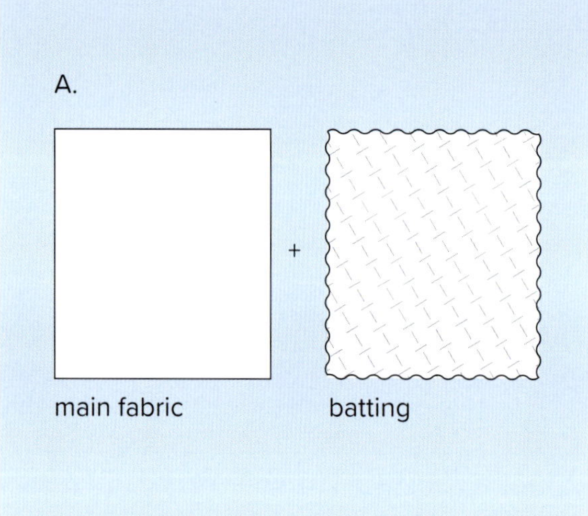

How to quilt fabric

A. Cut main fabric and batting to required size.

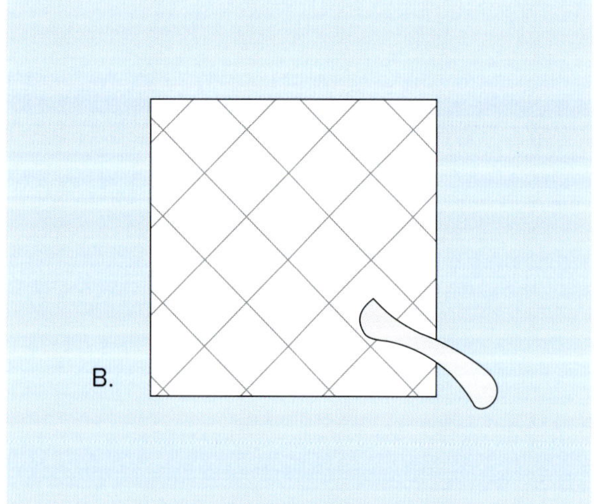

B. On right side of main fabric, mark quilting lines in your desired pattern with a hera marker and quilt ruler. This will create a crease line in your fabric to use as a guide when sewing. We use a 2-inch (5cm) diamond pattern.

C. Layer fabrics. With right side facing up, place main fabric on top of batting.

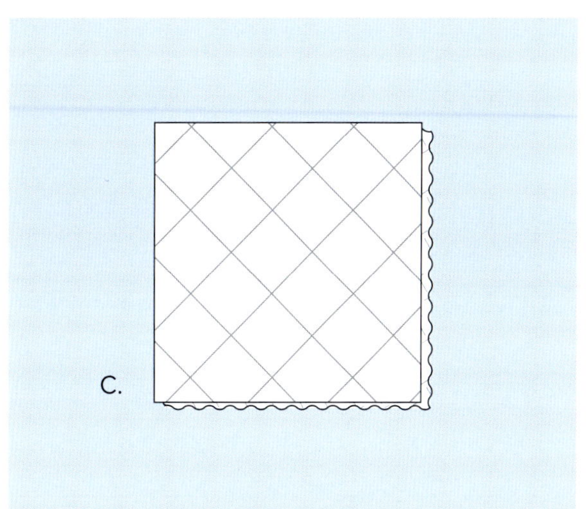

D. Make sure layers are flat and free of wrinkles. Pin layers together. With your walking foot attached and using a longer stitch length on your sewing machine (we use a stitch length of 3.4), stitch along the crease marks made in step B, removing pins as you go. Continue quilting in this method for all pattern pieces.

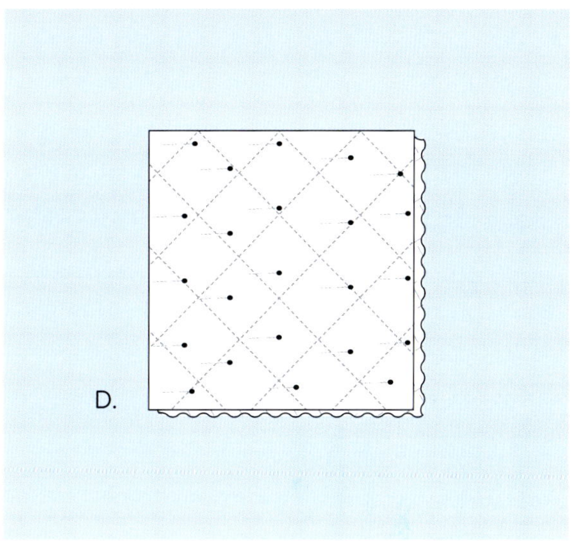

E. Lay pattern piece on top of newly quilted fabric. Cut around pattern piece through all the layers as normal.

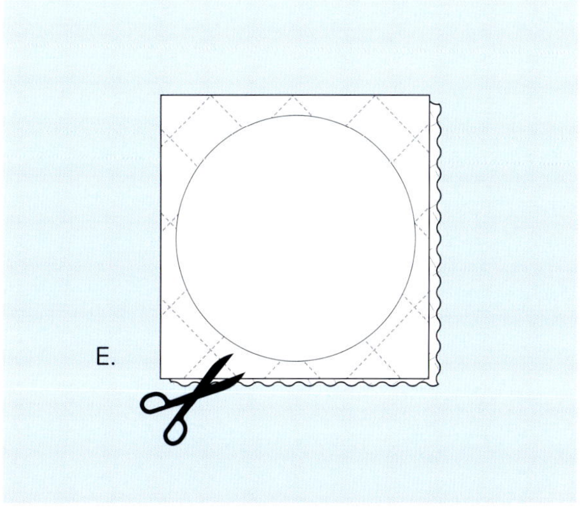

THE PROJECTS

TRIO TOP

The Trio Top is a simple, boxy top with only two pattern pieces, the perfect building block for creativity.

Skill level: Beginner

Techniques: Elastic channel, hemming

Fabric suggestions: Lightweight wovens such as linens or cottons

Notions: Coordinating thread, ¼-inch (0.6cm) elastic (optional)

Shape and Style

Boxy and loose.

Fit

Easy and flattering with a square neckline and elastic channel.

Three evenly divided pieces, making fabric choices a snap.

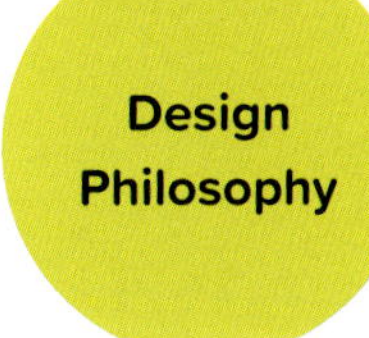

A nod to the classic visual principle known as the "rule of thirds."

Finished garment measurements (inch/cm)

	XXS	XS	S	M	L	XL
Chest	49 (124.5)	51 (129.5)	53 (135)	55 (140)	57½ (146)	60½ (154)
Hip/ Hem	49 (124.5)	51 (129.5)	53 (135)	55 (140)	57½ (146)	60½ (154)

	2XL	3XL	4XL	5XL	6XL
Chest	64½ (164)	68½ (174)	72½ (184)	76½ (194)	80½ (204)
Hip/ Hem	64½ (164)	68½ (174)	72½ (184)	76½ (194)	80½ (204)

Total fabric requirements (yard/m) Extra fabric may be needed to match stripes, plaids, or directional prints.

	Length (yard/m)					
Width	XXS	XS	S	M	L	XL
44in 112cm	1¼ 1.2	1¼ 1.2	1¼ 1.2	1¼ 1.2	1¼ 1.2	1½ 1.4
54in 137cm	1¼ 1.2	1¼ 1.2	1¼ 1.2	1¼ 1.2	1¼ 1.2	1½ 1.4

Width	2XL	3XL	4XL	5XL	6XL
44in 112cm	1½ 1.4	1½ 1.4	1½ 1.4	2½ 2.3	2½ 2.3
54in 137cm	1½ 1.4	1½ 1.4	1½ 1.4	1½ 1.4	1½ 1.4

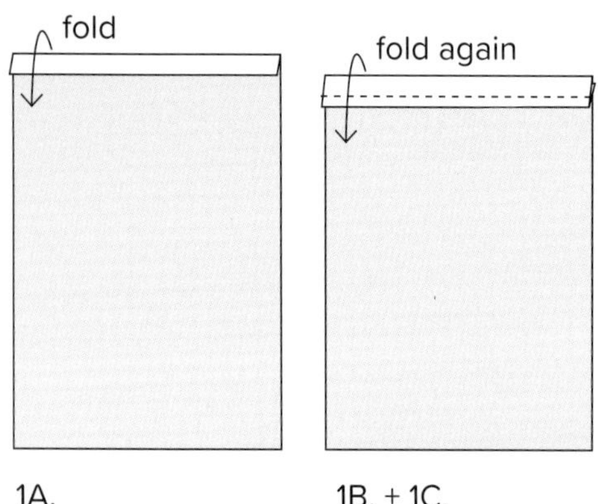

1A. 1B. + 1C.

1. Prepare center panels

A. Fold top raw edge by ¼ inch (0.6cm) toward wrong side of fabric. Press in place.

B. Fold by another ½ inch (1.3cm). Press in place.

C. Sew along bottom fold line using a ⅛-inch (0.3cm) seam allowance creating a channel for elastic.

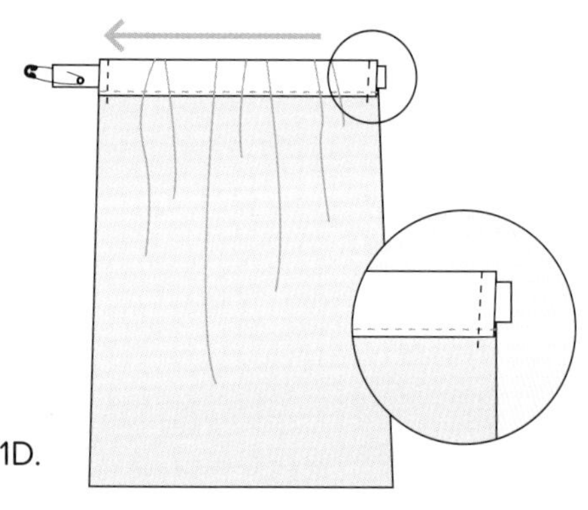

1D.

D. Cut two lengths of elastic according to size chart below. Attach safety pin to one end of elastic. Feed through channel until ½ inch (1.3cm) remains on one side. Sew using a ¼-inch (0.6cm) seam allowance to secure elastic in place. Pull elastic until it comes out the other side by ½ inch (1.3cm). Sew using a ¼-inch (0.6cm) seam allowance to secure in place. Remove safety pin. Trim any extra elastic.

Elastic length

	XXS	XS	S	M	L	XL
IN	7½	7¾	8	8¼	8½	8¾
CM	19	19.8	20.5	21	21.5	22.3
	2XL	**3XL**	**4XL**	**5XL**	**6XL**	
IN	9	9¼	9½	9¾	10	
CM	23	23.5	24	24.8	25.5	

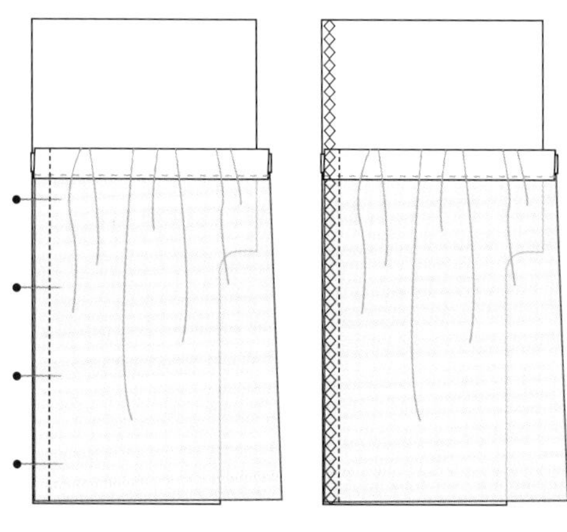

2A. + 2B.

2. Attach side panels

A. With right sides together, match side panel to center panel aligning at hem. Pin in place. Sew with a ½-inch (1.3cm) seam allowance.

B. Finish entire center seam from shoulder to bottom hem with a zigzag stitch or serger.

Finishing stitch will not be illustrated in future steps.

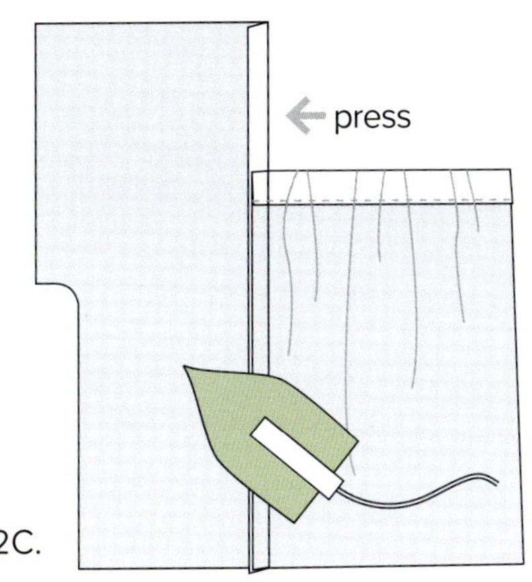

C. Press seam toward side panel, continuing up to the shoulder seam using the ½-inch (1.3cm) seam allowance as a guide. Unfold at shoulder. This press mark will serve as a guide in a later step. Repeat steps 2A–2C for other side panel. Repeat all steps for back body. You now have a completed front body and a completed back body.

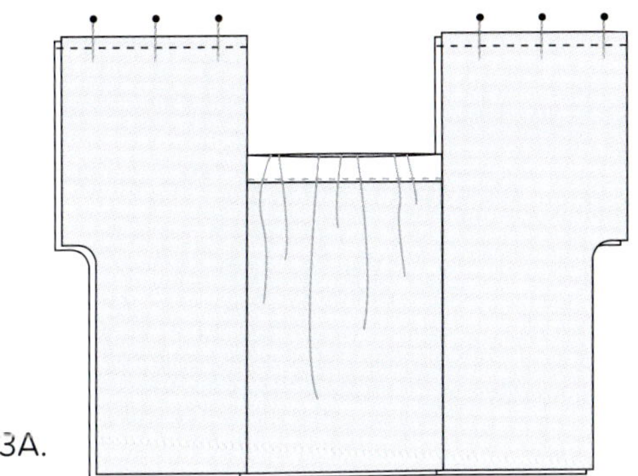

3. Sew shoulder seams

A. With right sides together, align front and back shoulder seams. Make sure pressed seam made in step 2C stays unfolded so that shoulder seams match exactly. Pin in place. Sew with a ½-inch (1.3cm) seam allowance. Finish seam with a zigzag stitch or serger. Press seam toward back. Do this for both shoulders.

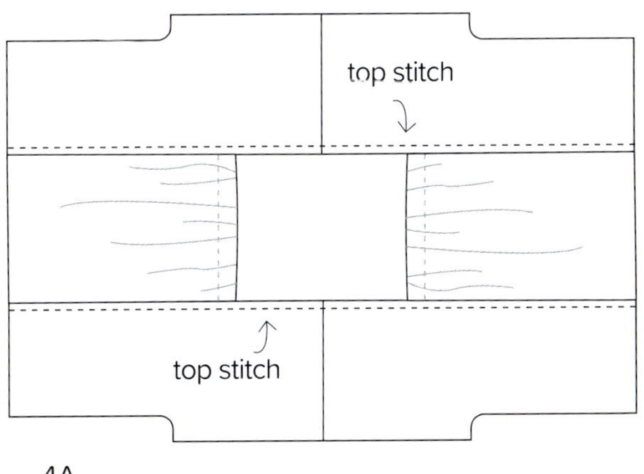

4. Top stitching

A. Open garment flat with right side facing up. Make sure all center seam allowances and press marks made in step 2C are still pressed toward the side panels. Re-press if needed. Top stitch using a ¼-inch (0.6cm) seam allowance on either side of the center panel from back hem to front hem, making sure to catch all the seam allowances beneath.

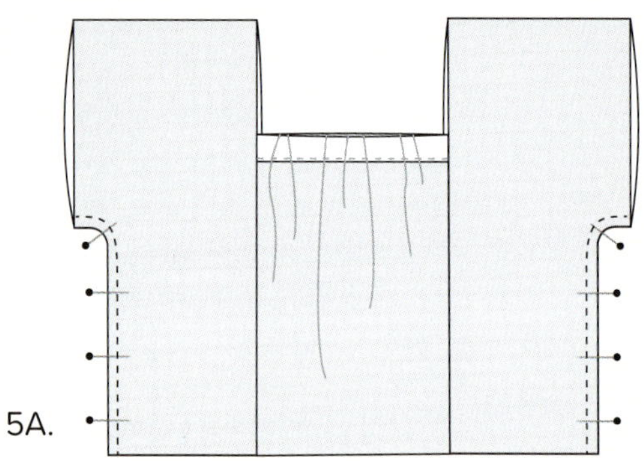

5. Sew side seams

A. With right sides together, align front and back side seams. Pin in place. Sew with a ½-inch (1.3cm) seam allowance. Finish with a zigzag stitch or serger. Press seam toward back. Repeat for both side seams.

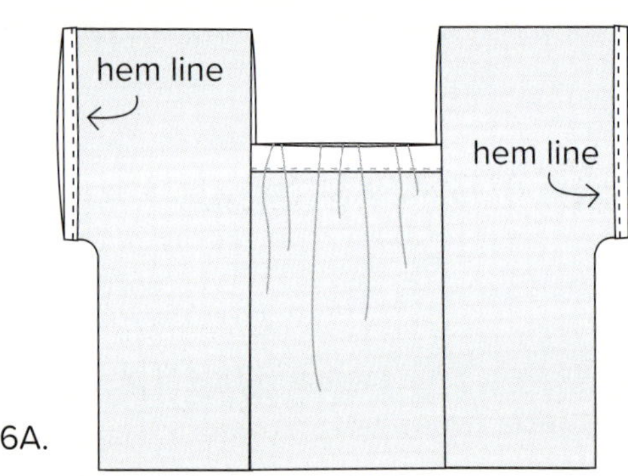

6. Hem sleeves

A. Fold sleeve hem ¼ inch (0.6cm) toward wrong side. Press in place. Fold again by another ¼ inch (0.6cm). Press and pin in place. Sew ⅛ inch (0.3cm) away from the folded edge. Repeat for other sleeve.

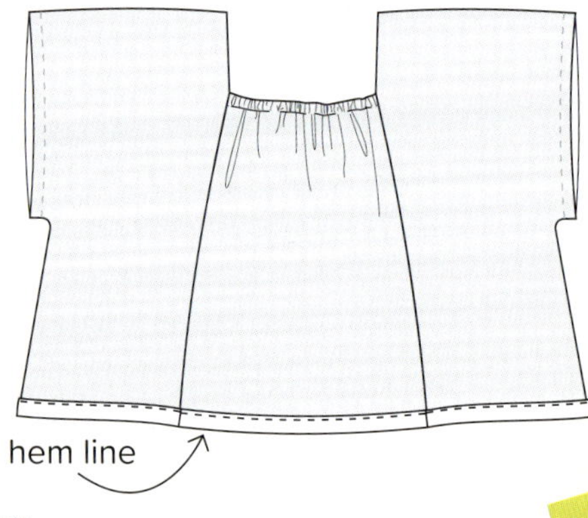

7. Hem bottom

A. Fold bottom hem ½ inch (1.3cm) toward wrong side. Press in place. Fold again by another ½ inch (1.3cm). Press and pin in place. Sew ⅛ inch (0.3cm) away from the folded edge.

For details on hemming see page 40.

Congrats, you've completed the first project!

COLOR STRATEGY

COMPLEMENTARY

TRIO TOP

Why it works

Blue and yellow are complementary colors, which gives this palette a bold, energetic feel. The addition of black as a neutral helps ground the contrast and tie everything together.

Tip

Dividing the colors into three equal sections keeps the balance, making the patchwork feel intentional and harmonious.

TRIO DRESS

The Trio Dress is a fresh mini dress that will give you the skills to turn any top into a new garment.

Skill level: Beginner

Techniques: Gathering, hemming

Fabric suggestions: Lightweight wovens such as linens or cottons

Notions: Coordinating thread, ¼-inch (0.6cm) elastic (optional)

Shape and Style

Square shapes with a short, sassy gathered skirt.

Fit

Easy-fitting mini dress with a square neckline and high waistline.

Construction

As simple as can be with an adorable, flattering shape.

Design Philosophy

Building on basic garments is the best way to gain skills and expand your wardrobe.

Finished garment measurements (inch/cm)

	XXS	XS	S	M	L	XL
Chest	42 (107)	44 (112)	46 (117)	48 (122)	50½ (128)	53½ (136)
Hip/ Hem	63 (160)	66 (168)	69 (175)	72 (183)	76 (193)	80 (203)

	2XL	3XL	4XL	5XL	6XL
Chest	57½ (146)	61½ (156)	65½ (166)	69½ (176)	73½ (186)
Hip/ Hem	86 (218)	92 (234)	98 (249)	104 (264)	110 (279)

Total fabric requirements (yard/m) Extra fabric may be needed to match stripes, plaids, or directional prints.

	Length (yard/m)					
Width	XXS	XS	S	M	L	XL
44in 112cm	2½ 2.3	2½ 2.3	2½ 2.3	2½ 2.3	3¼ 3	3¼ 3
54in 137cm	2½ 2.3	2½ 2.3	2½ 2.3	2½ 2.3	2¾ 2.6	2¾ 2.6

Width	2XL	3XL	4XL	5XL	6XL
44in 112cm	3¼ 3	3¼ 3	4¼ 3.9	4¼ 3.9	4¼ 3.9
54in 137cm	2¾ 2.6	2¾ 2.6	3½ 3.3	3½ 3.3	3½ 3.3

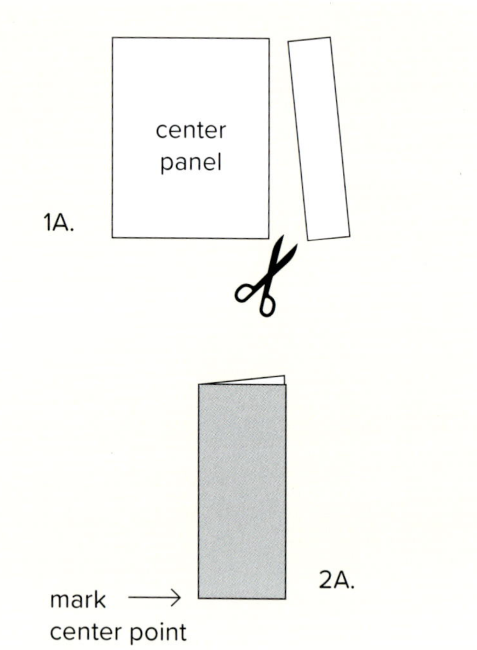

Skirt width x 25 inches (63.5cm) high

	XXS	XS	S	M	L	XL
IN	31½	33	34½	36	38	40
CM	80	84	87.5	91.5	96.5	101.5
	2XL	**3XL**	**4XL**	**5XL**	**6XL**	
IN	43	46	49	52	55	
CM	109	117	124.5	132	140	

Add or subtract width to increase or reduce fullness. Add or subtract height to lengthen or shorten dress length.

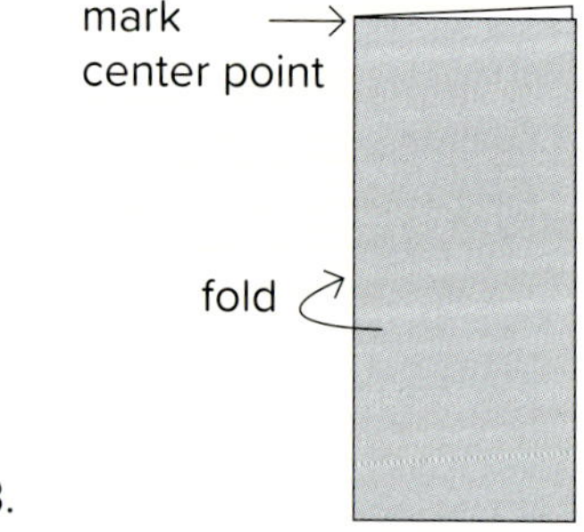

1. Adjust paper pattern

A. The Trio Top and Dress can be sewn with or without elastic in the center panel. To make the dress without elastic, first adjust the paper pattern by cutting 1¾ inches (4.5cm) off one side of the center panel. Use this new pattern piece when cutting fabric. Remember, you will still be cutting this piece on the fold.

2. Prepare bodice

A. Find center point of center panel by folding panel in half widthwise. Make a small notch on the bottom edge. Do this for both front and back center panels.

B. Continue to follow the same method from the Trio Top instructions on page 50, using steps 1A–1C. Skip step 1D (the step for inserting elastic) and continue with steps 2–6. Instead of hemming, let's add a skirt to turn this cute top into a mini dress.

3. Prepare skirt

A. Piece together fabric scraps or use a single piece of fabric (some sizes will require two lengths to be joined). Cut final fabric piece to meet the measurement in the chart above left. You will need two pieces of fabric this size.

B. Find center point of skirt by folding skirt panel in half widthwise. Make a mark with a small notch or pin. Do this for both skirt panels.

TRIO DRESS

COLOR STRATEGY

MONOCHROMATIC WITH DENIM

Why it works

Using an all-denim monochromatic palette creates a look that's cohesive and timeless. Mixing light, medium, and dark washes adds just the right amount of contrast, keeping the patchwork visually interesting without feeling too busy.

Tip

Using all denim keeps the texture consistent, which helps unify your patchwork even when the colors vary.

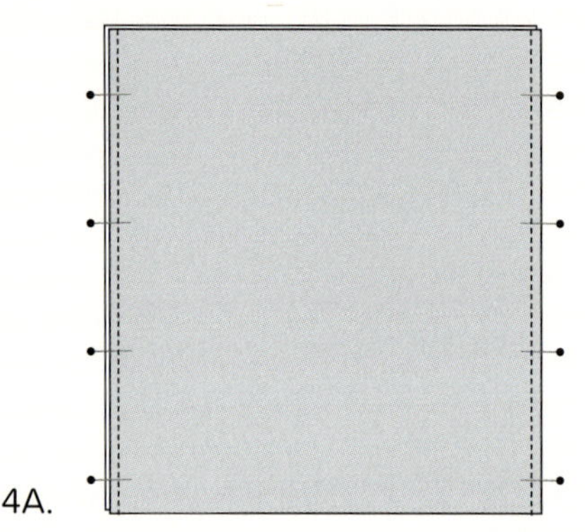

4A.

4. Sew side seams

A. With right sides together, align front and back skirt panels at side seams. Pin in place. Sew both side seams using a ½-inch (1.3cm) seam allowance. Finish seam with a zigzag stitch or serger. Press seams toward back.

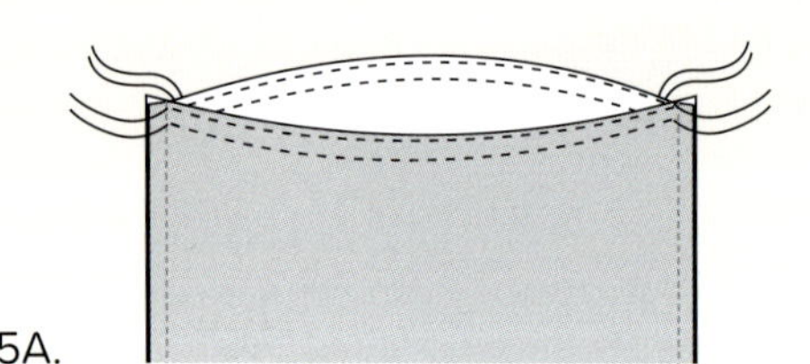

5A.

5B.

5. Gather and attach skirt

A. To gather skirt, follow instructions on page 39 on how to gather. Gather front and back skirt separately, starting and stopping just before the side seams.

B. With right sides together, align gathered edge of skirt to bottom edge of body, matching at center notches and side seams. Evenly distribute gathers and pin in place. Sew with a ½-inch (1.3cm) seam allowance. Remove visible gathering stitches. Finish seam with a zigzag stitch or serger. Press seam toward body.

6A.

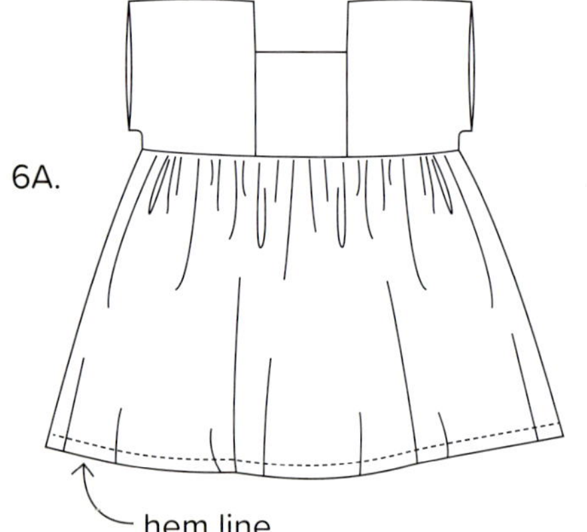

6. Hem skirt

A. Fold bottom hem ½ inch (1.3cm) toward wrong side. Press in place. Fold again by another ½ inch (1.3cm). Press and pin in place. Sew ⅛ inch (0.3cm) away from the folded edge.

For details on hemming see page 40.

GARDENER SKIRT

The Gardener Skirt is a great project for beginners with simple shapes and no pattern pieces to assemble.

Skill level: Beginner

Techniques: Elastic channel

Fabric suggestions: Light to midweight wovens such as linens or cottons

Notions: Coordinating thread, 1½-inch (4cm) wide elastic

Shape and Style

A mid-length skirt that is gathered at the waist with dramatic oversized side pockets.

Fit

Relaxed and easy with an elastic waist.

Construction

No pattern pieces required, just cut rectangles of fabric to size with flexible possibilities.

Design Philosophy

Simple shapes can create dramatic results—and there's always room for pockets!

Finished garment measurements (inch/cm)

	XXS	XS	S	M	L	XL
	Waist—self determined Length—31 inches (79cm)					
Hip/ Hem	56 (142)	58 (147)	60 (152)	62 (157)	64½ (164)	67½ (171)

	2XL	3XL	4XL	5XL	6XL
	Waist—self determined Length—31 inches (79cm)				
Hip/ Hem	71 (180)	75½ (192)	79½ (202)	83½ (212)	87½ (222)

Total fabric requirements (yard/m) Extra fabric may be needed to match stripes, plaids, or directional prints.

	Length (yard/m)					
Width	XXS	XS	S	M	L	XL
44in 112cm	2¾ 2.6	2¾ 2.6	2¾ 2.6	2¾ 2.6	2¾ 2.6	2¾ 2.6
54in 137cm	2¾ 2.6	2¾ 2.6	2¾ 2.6	2¾ 2.6	2¾ 2.6	2¾ 2.6

Width	2XL	3XL	4XL	5XL	6XL
44in 112cm	2¾ 2.6	2¾ 2.6	3¾ 3.5	3¾ 3.5	3¾ 3.5
54in 137cm	2¾ 2.6	2¾ 2.6	2¾ 2.6	2¾ 2.6	2¾ 2.6

PATTERN PIECE MEASUREMENTS

Front side panel

Width x 53½ inches (136cm) high

	XXS	XS	S	M	L	XL
IN	10	10¼	10¾	11	11½	12
CM	25.5	26	27.3	28	29.3	30.5

	2XL	3XL	4XL	5XL	6XL
IN	12½	13¼	13¾	14½	15
CM	31.8	33.8	35	37	38

Front center panel

Width x 35½ inches (90cm) high

	XXS	XS	S	M	L	XL
IN	11	11¼	11¾	12	12⅜	13
CM	28	28.5	29.8	30.5	31.5	33

	2XL	3XL	4XL	5XL	6XL
IN	13½	14¼	14¾	15⅜	16
CM	34.3	36	37.5	39	40.5

Back panel

Width x 35½ inches (90cm) high

	XXS	XS	S	M	L	XL
IN	29	30	31	32	34	35
CM	73.5	76.3	78.8	81.3	86.4	88.9

	2XL	3XL	4XL	5XL	6XL
IN	37	39	41	43	45
CM	94	99.1	104.2	109.2	114.3

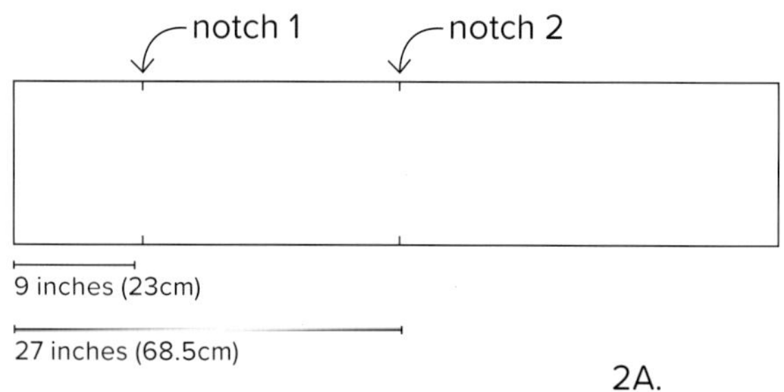

2A.

1. Cut fabric

A. Piece together fabric scraps or use a single piece of fabric. Cut final fabric pieces to meet the measurements in the charts to the left. You will need two front side panels, one front center panel, and one back panel.

2. Make side panel pockets

A. To find pocket notches, measure 9 inches (23cm) down from top of side panel. Cut a ¼-inch (0.6cm) notch on both sides. This will be the first set of notches. Measure again 27 inches (68.5cm) down from top of side panel. Cut a ¼-inch (0.6cm) notch on both sides. This will be the second set of notches.

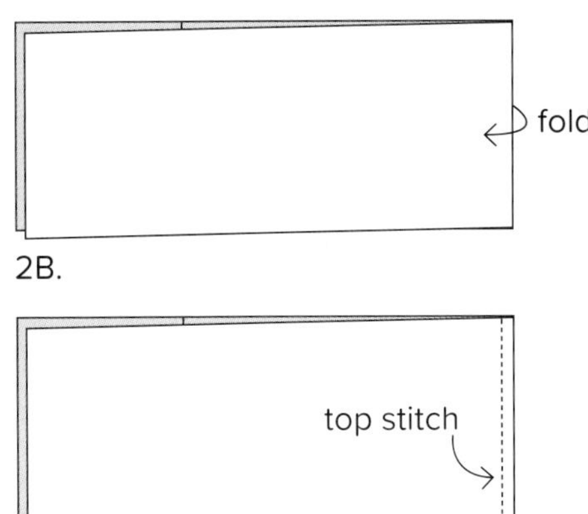

2B.

2C.

B. Fold fabric in half at second notch with wrong sides together. Press in place.

C. Topstitch at folded end through both layers with a ¼-inch (0.6cm) seam allowance.

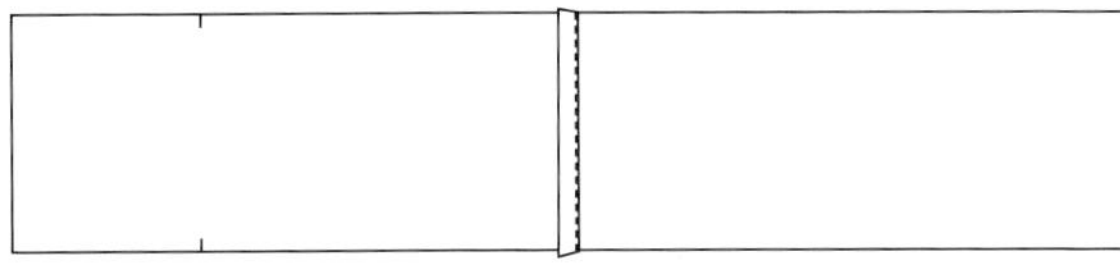

2D.

D. Open panel back up.

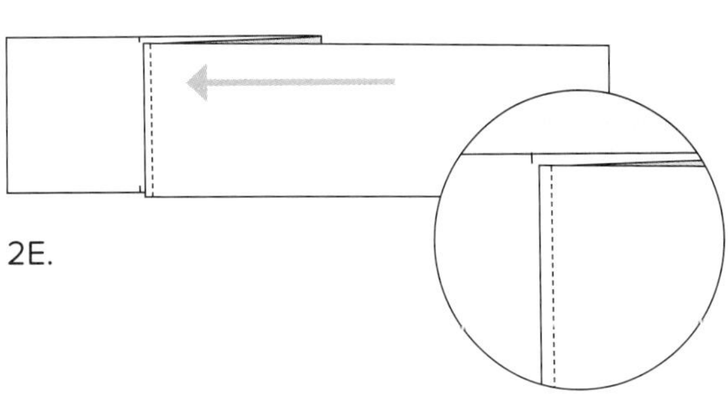

2E.

E. With right side facing up, pull folded sewn edge up to meet the top set of notches. Press in place.

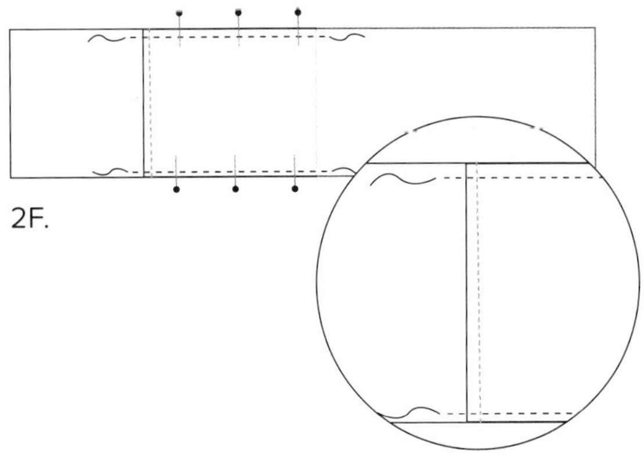

2F.

F. Pin in place. Temporarily secure with a basting stitch on both sides, using a ¼-inch (0.6cm) seam allowance. Repeat steps 2A–2F for other side panel pocket.

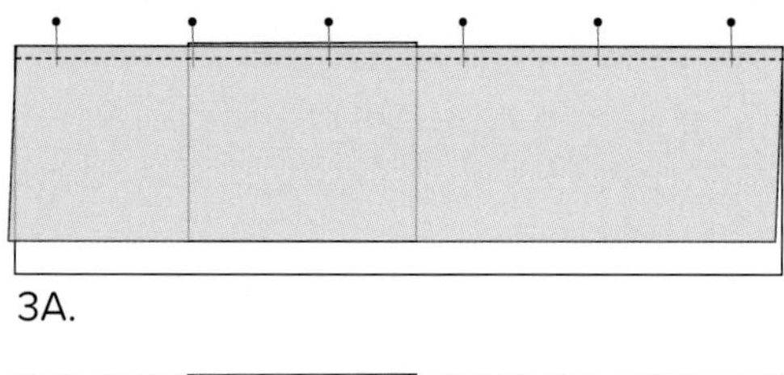

3A.

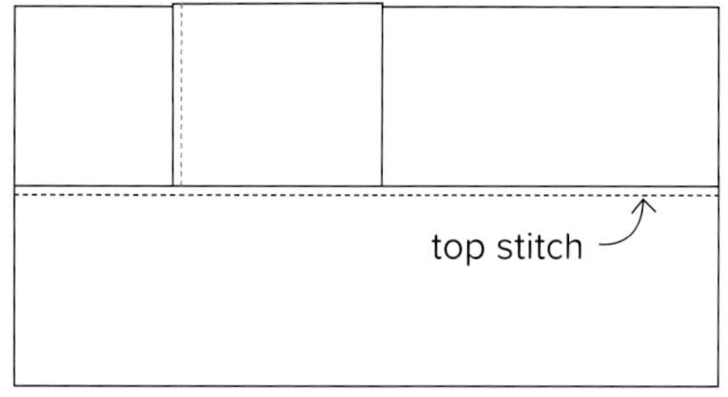

3B.

3. Attach front skirt panels

A. With right sides together, align side panel to center panel, making sure pocket opening is pointing up. Pin in place. Sew with a ½-inch (1.3cm) seam allowance. Finish seam with a zigzag stitch or serger. Press seam toward center panel.

B. Top stitch on center panel using a ¼-inch (0.6cm) seam allowance, making sure to catch all the seam allowances beneath. Repeat steps 3A–3B for other side panel. Your front skirt panel is now complete.

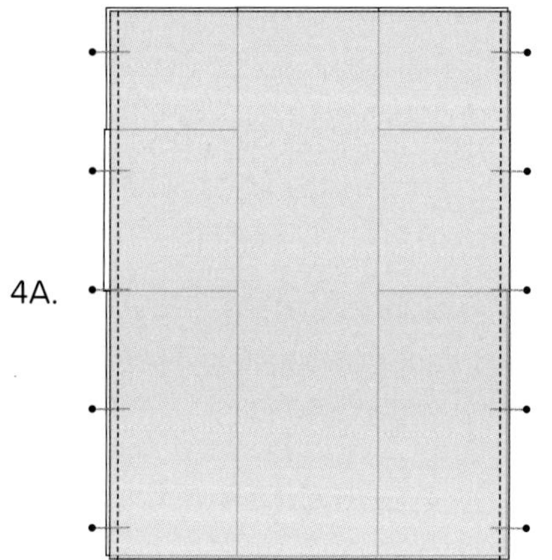

4A.

4. Attach front and back panels

A. With right sides together, align completed front skirt to back skirt panel at side seams. Pin in place. If front and back skirt panel lengths are uneven, trim to match. Don't worry if the width of front and back panels are not exactly the same, it will all work out. Sew both side seams using a ½-inch (1.3cm) seam allowance. Finish seam with a zigzag stitch or serger. Press seams toward back.

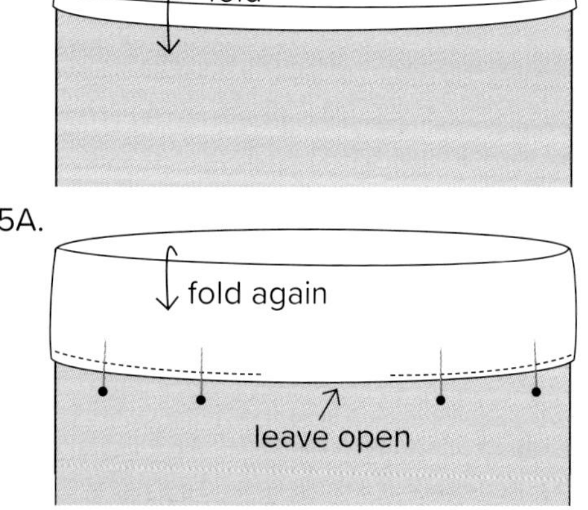

5A.

5. Complete waistband

A. Fold top raw edge over by ½ inch (1.3cm) toward wrong side. Press in place. Fold over again by 1¾ inches (4.5cm) toward wrong side. Press and pin in place. Edge stitch using a ⅛-inch (0.3cm) seam allowance along the bottom folded edge leaving a 4-inch (10cm) opening at center back. This forms a channel for elastic.

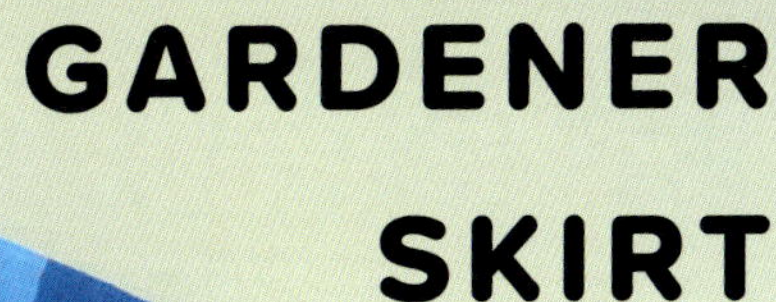

GARDENER SKIRT

COLOR STRATEGY

ANALOGOUS WITH MINIMAL COLORS

Why it works

Analogous colors—like blue and green—sit next to each other on the color wheel, creating a sense of calm and harmony. Introducing a pattern like a wide stripe will inject interest and movement.

Tip

Sticking to just two colors is an easy way to build confidence with mixing fabrics.

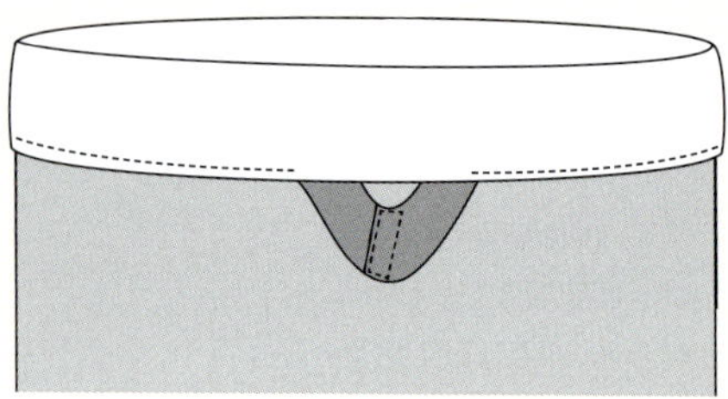
5B.

B. Without stretching it, cut a piece of 1½-inch (4cm) wide elastic to a length that fits comfortably around your waist, plus 1 inch (2.5cm) extra. Attach a safety pin to one end of the elastic and feed it through the opening of the waistband channel, making sure it does not get twisted along the way. When the two elastic ends meet, overlap by 1 inch (2.5cm), pin in place, and sew the elastic together, forming a rectangle. Backstitch to secure.

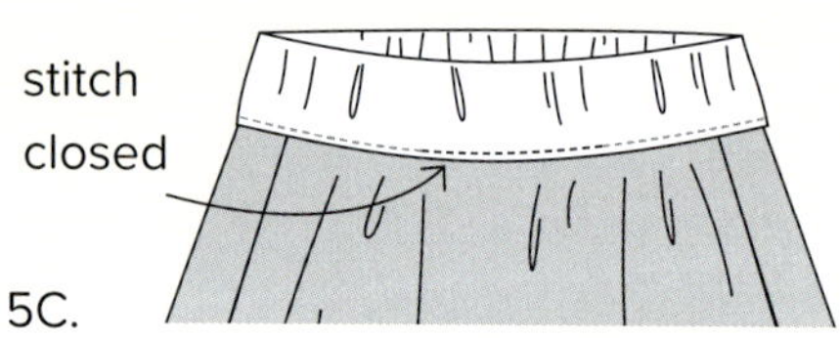

5C.

C. Stitch back waistband opening closed, being careful not to stitch through elastic. Distribute elastic around channel so the gathering is even.

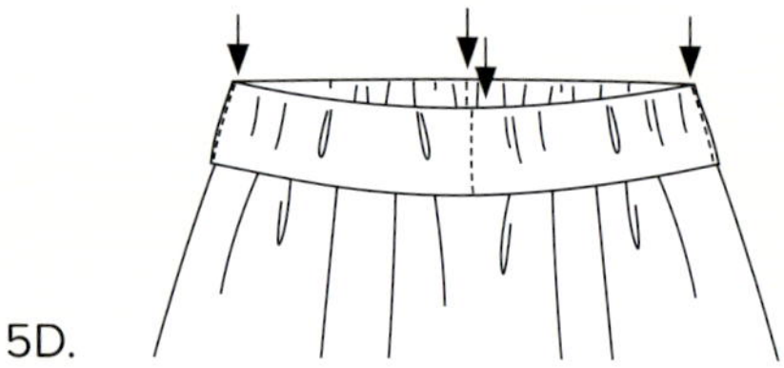
5D.

D. With garment right side out, sew vertical lines through all layers of waistband at center front, center back, and side seams. This will keep elastic in place during wear and washing.

6A.

6. Hem skirt

A. Fold bottom hem ½ inch (1.3cm) toward wrong side. Press in place. Fold again by another 1½ inches (4cm). Press and pin in place. Sew ⅛ inch (0.3cm) away from the folded edge.

For details on hemming see page 40.

Look, a skirt with pockets made from rectangles!

RUFFLE HAND-KERCHIEF

The Ruffle Handkerchief is a fast and fun quilting project for beginners.

Skill level: Beginner

Techniques: Quilting, gathering

Fabric suggestions: Light to midweight wovens such as linens, cottons, flannel

Batting: Lightweight cotton batting. We use the brand "Warm & Natural" cotton batting

Notions: Coordinating thread

Shape and Style

Triangular shape that gracefully drapes over the shoulders, adorned with a sweet and frilly ruffle trim along the outer edge.

Fit

The back drops just past shoulder blades, the front accommodates easy tying.

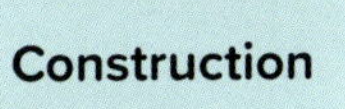

Construction

Quilted, lined, simple.

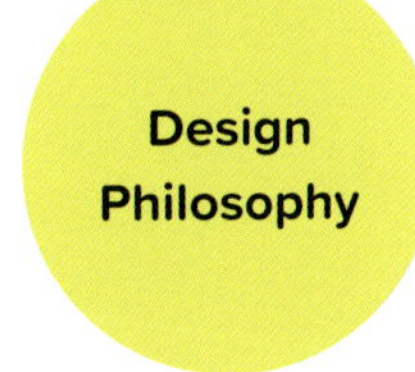

Design Philosophy

Cozy with a touch of fun.

Finished garment measurements (inch/cm)

46 x 14 inches (116.9 x 35.6cm)

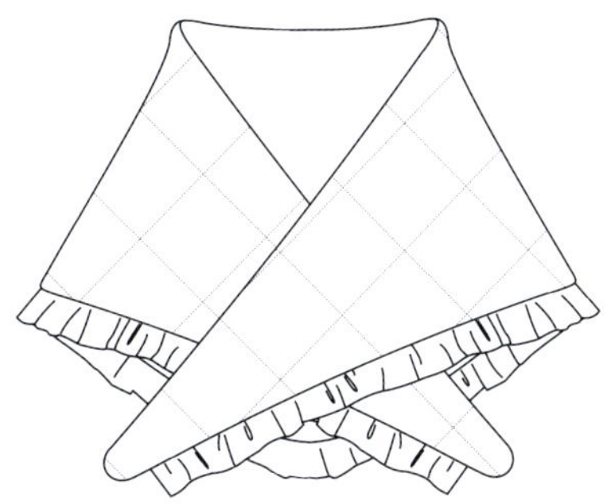

Total fabric requirements (inch/cm)

Extra fabric may be needed to match stripes, plaids, or directional prints.

Fabric	W x H	Total Qty
Main	44 x 16 (112 x 40.5)	cut 1
Lining	44 x 16 (112 x 40.5)	cut 1
Batting	44 x 16 (112 x 40.5)	cut 1
Ruffle	36 x 3 (91.5 x 7.8)	cut 2

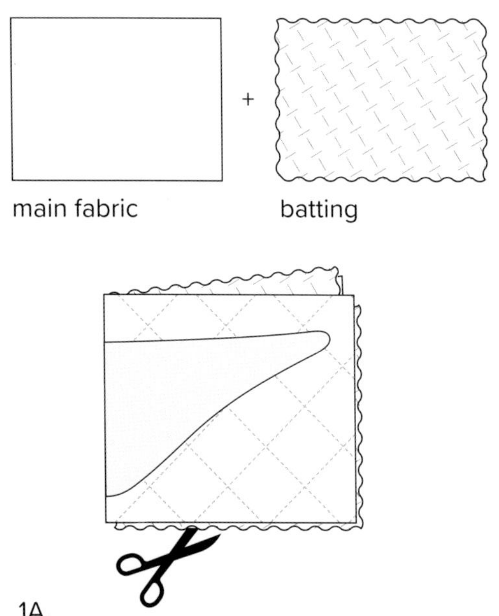

1A.

1. Quilt main fabric

A. Cut one main fabric and one batting fabric according to the measurements in the measurement chart. Follow the quilting instructions on page 44 to quilt the main fabric to the batting. Fold quilted piece in half lengthwise and cut pattern piece out on the fold. Mark bottom center point with small notch.

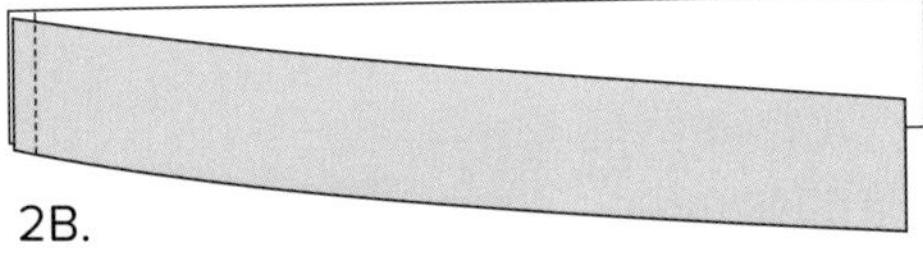
2B.

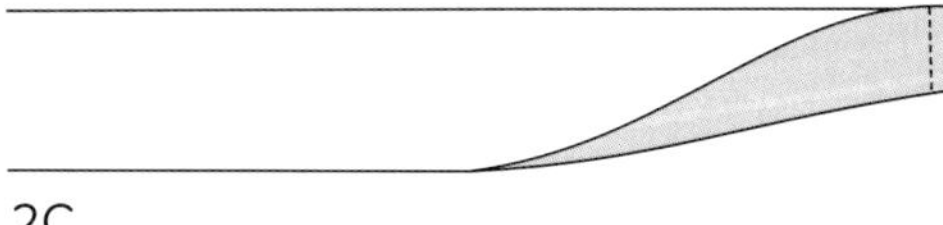
2C.

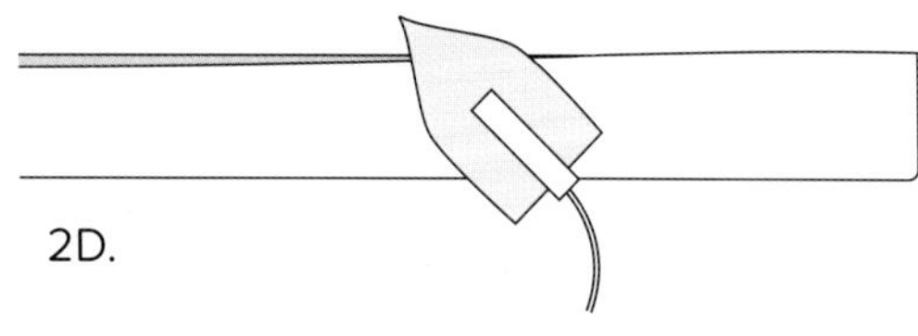
2D.

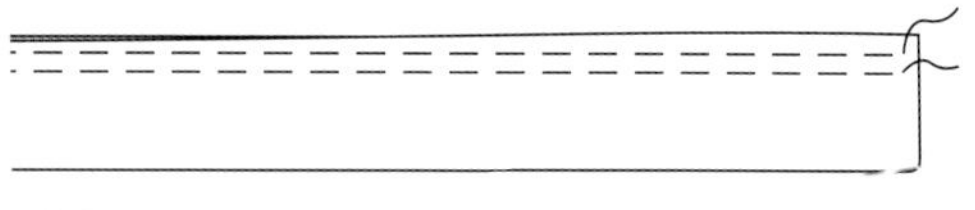
2E.

2. Prepare ruffle

A. Cut ruffle pieces according to the measurements in the measurement chart.

B. With right sides together, match one of the short ends from the two ruffle pieces. Sew with a ½-inch (1.3cm) seam allowance. Press seam open, forming a long strip.

C. With right sides together fold the short ends in half. Sew with a ½-inch (1.3cm) seam allowance on both short ends.

D. Flip ruffle so that right side faces out. Use a long sharp object, such as a knitting needle, to push out the corner to a point. Press in half along entire strip. Raw ends on short ends are now enclosed.

E. With ruffle still folded, follow the gathering instructions on page 39 to gather the raw edges of folded ruffle.

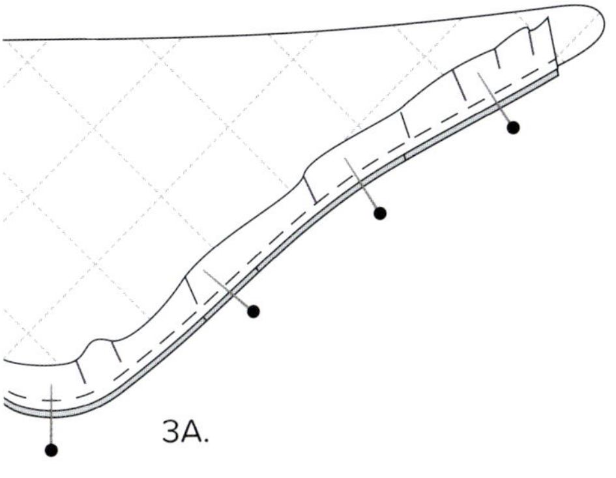

3. Attach ruffle

A. With right sides together, match gathered raw edge of ruffle to outer edge of the handkerchief, starting and stopping at the two corner notches. The center seam of the ruffle will match the bottom center notch on the handkerchief. Distribute gathers evenly. Pin in place. Temporarily hold ruffle in place by sewing a basting stitch using a ¼-inch (0.6cm) seam allowance. Remove any visible basting stitches.

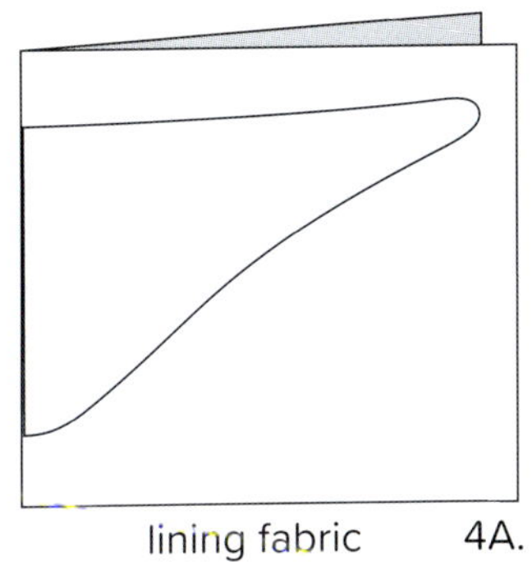

4. Sew lining

A. Fold lining fabric in half lengthwise and cut pattern piece out on the fold.

B. With right sides together, layer lining fabric to main fabric. The ruffle will be sandwiched in between. Pin around entire perimeter. Sew using a ½-inch (1.3cm) seam allowance, starting and stopping 4 inches (10cm) from center back and leaving an opening for turning your handkerchief right side out.

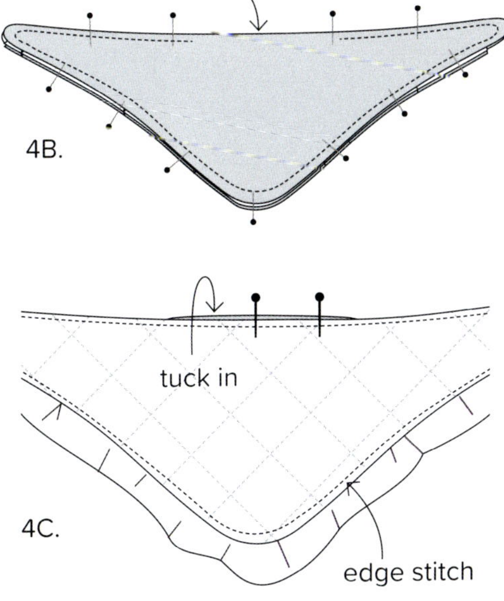

C. To make turning easier, trim seam allowances around curved edges to ¼ inch (0.6cm) then flip handkerchief to the right side through center back opening. Tuck in raw edges of opening toward inside of handkerchief using the ½-inch (1.3cm) seam allowance as a guide. Pin opening closed. Edge stitch using a ⅛-inch (0.3cm) seam allowance around entire handkerchief, closing the opening in the process.

Tidy your ruffles, and snuggle up in your new handkerchief!

SPRING BUTTON-UP

The Spring Button-Up will build confidence in the skills you've already learned, with a few new ones added along the way.

Skill level: Confident beginner

Techniques: Sleeves, patch pockets, bias binding, buttonholes & buttons

Fabric suggestions: Light to midweight wovens such as linens, cottons, denim

Notions: Coordinating thread, five ½-inch (1.3cm) buttons, fusible interfacing (optional)

Shape and Style

Boxy with crew neckline, front button placket, bracelet length sleeves, and optional front patch pockets.

Fit

Relaxed with dropped shoulders, and hits at the hip.

Construction

Easy to sew with maximum patchwork possibilities.

Design Philosophy

Elevated personality for your wardrobe essentials.

Finished garment measurements (inch/cm)

	XXS	XS	S	M	L	XL
Chest	41½ (105)	43½ (110)	45½ (115.5)	47½ (121)	50 (127)	53 (135)
Hip/ Hem	41½ (105)	43½ (110)	45½ (115.5)	47½ (121)	50 (127)	53 (135)

	2XL	3XL	4XL	5XL	6XL
Chest	57 (145)	61 (155)	65 (165)	69 (175)	73 (185)
Hip/ Hem	57 (145)	61 (155)	65 (165)	69 (175)	73 (185)

Total fabric requirements (yard/m) Extra fabric may be needed to match stripes, plaids, or directional prints.

	Length (yard/m)					
Width	XXS	XS	S	M	L	XL
44in 112cm	2¼ 2.1	2¼ 2.1	2¼ 2.1	2¼ 2.1	2¾ 2.6	2¾ 2.6
54in 137cm	2 1.9	2 1.9	2 1.9	2 1.9	2 1.9	2 1.9

Width	2XL	3XL	4XL	5XL	6XL
44in 112cm	2¾ 2.6	3 2.8	3 2.8	3 2.8	3 2.8
54in 137cm	2 1.9	2½ 2.3	2½ 2.3	3 2.8	3 2.8

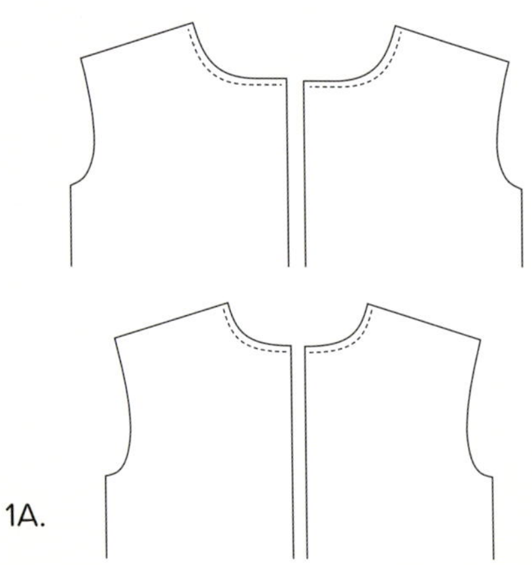

1. Staystitch

A. Staystitch front and back necklines (refer to page 38 on how to staystitch).

1A.

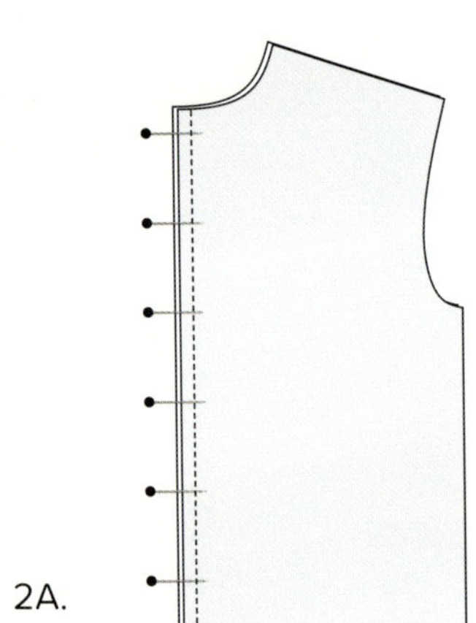

2. Piece back body

A. With right sides together, pin back bodice panels together at center back. Sew with a ½-inch (1.3cm) seam allowance. Finish with a zigzag stitch or serger. Press seam toward one side.

2A.

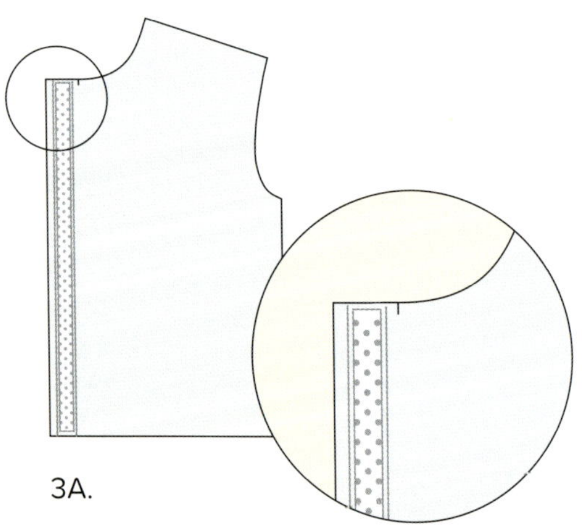

3. Prepare front button placket

A. Cut two pieces of fusible interfacing 1 inch (2.5cm) wide by length of center front panel. Apply to wrong side of fabric between fold lines on both left and right fronts. This step is optional but we do recommend it if using a lightweight fabric.

3A.

Quick tip: *Fusible interfacing is a thin, adhesive-backed material that's used to add structure and stability. Our preferred brand is Pellon 101 Shape-Flex, which is a woven interfacing.*

COLOR STRATEGY

SCRAPPY COMPLEMENTARY

SPRING BUTTON-UP

Tip

Find balance by having equal amounts of light, medium, and dark fabrics.

Why it works

The complementary colors blue and orange create balance. Softer neutrals—like sage green—expand the value range, while the stripes add texture and interest.

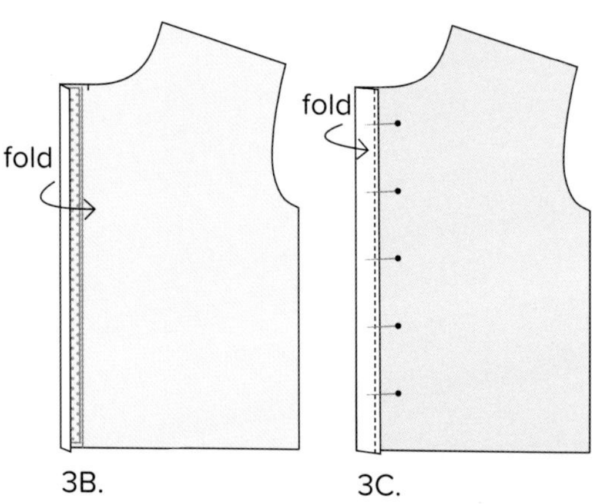

B. Fold the center front ½ inch (1.3cm) toward the wrong side. Press in place.

C. Fold over again 1 inch (2.5cm) toward the wrong side, covering the interfacing. Press and pin in place. Edge stitch ⅛ inch (0.3cm) away from folded edge. Repeat steps 3B–3C for other front panel.

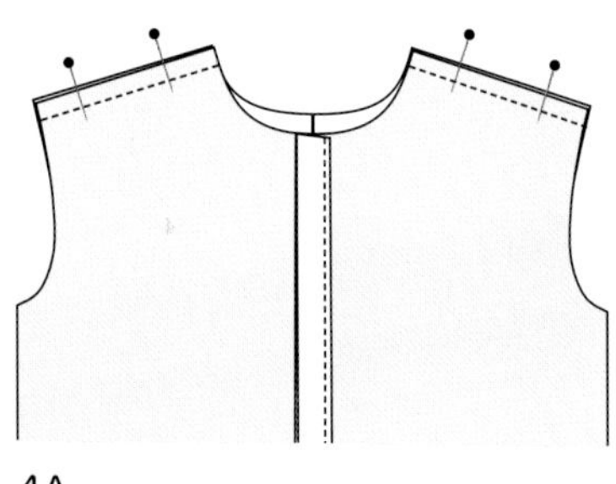

4. Sew shoulder seams

A. With right sides together, pin front and back shoulders. Sew with a ½-inch (1.3cm) seam allowance. Finish seam with a zigzag stitch or serger. Press seams toward back.

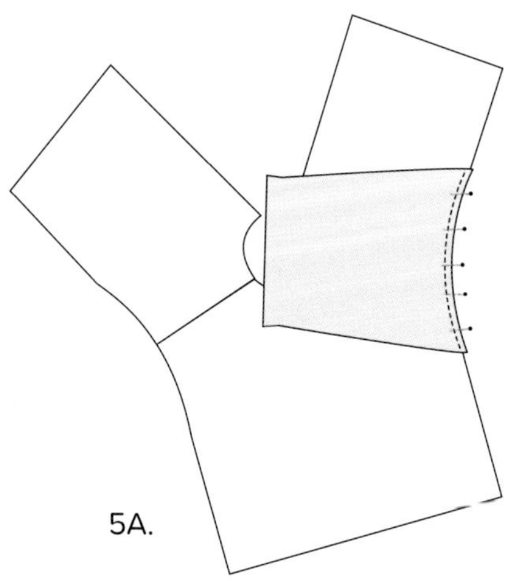

5. Attach sleeves

A. With right sides together, align sleeve to armhole, matching at notches. The center notch will align with shoulder seam. Sew with a ½-inch (1.3cm) seam allowance. Finish seam with a zigzag stitch or serger. Press seam toward sleeve, then repeat for other sleeve.

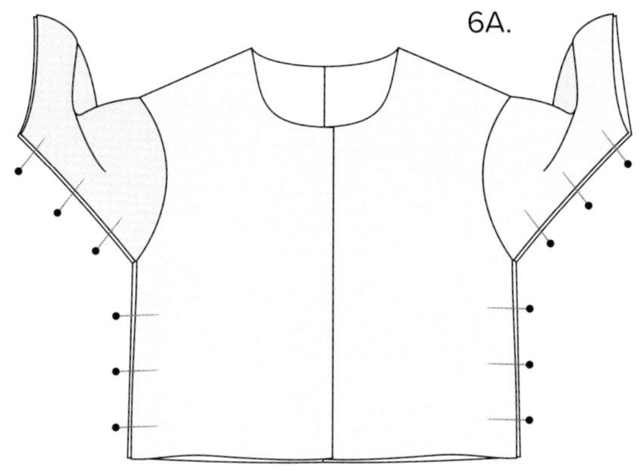

6. Sew side seams

A. With right sides together, match front and back side seams, aligning at underarm seam. Sew with a ½-inch (1.3cm) seam allowance. Finish seam with a zigzag stitch or serger. Press seam toward back. Repeat for other side.

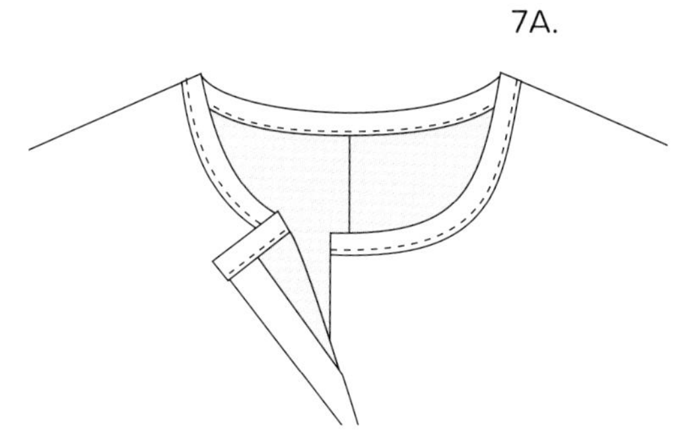

7. Attach neckline bias binding

A. Cut one length of bias according to measurement chart below. Continue following finished end bias binding method on page 33.

Neckline bias length **x 1⅝ inches (4cm) high**

	XXS	XS	S	M	L	XL
IN	23	23¾	24½	25¼	26	26¾
CM	58.5	60.5	62.3	64.3	66	68

	2XL	3XL	4XL	5XL	6XL
IN	27½	28¼	29	29¾	30½
CM	70	71.8	73.8	75.5	77.5

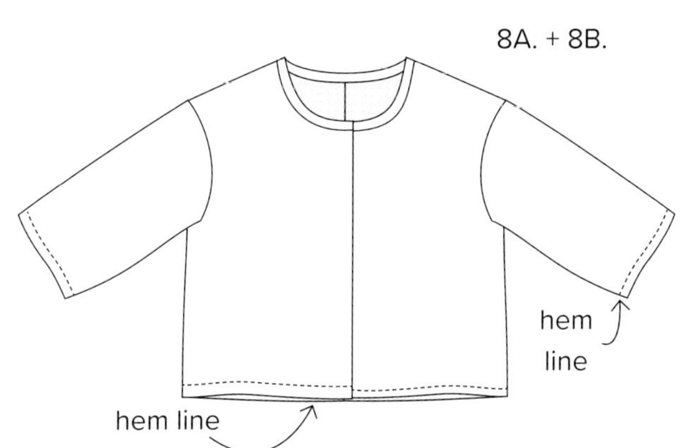

8. Hem sleeves and body

A. To hem the sleeves, press the raw edge of sleeve hem under by ½ inch (1.3cm) toward wrong side. Press under again by another ½ inch (1.3cm). Pin in place and sew along folded line.

B. To hem the body, press the bottom raw edge under by ½ inch (1.3cm) toward the wrong side. Press under again by another ½ inch (1.3cm). Pin in place and sew along folded line.

For details on hemming see page 40.

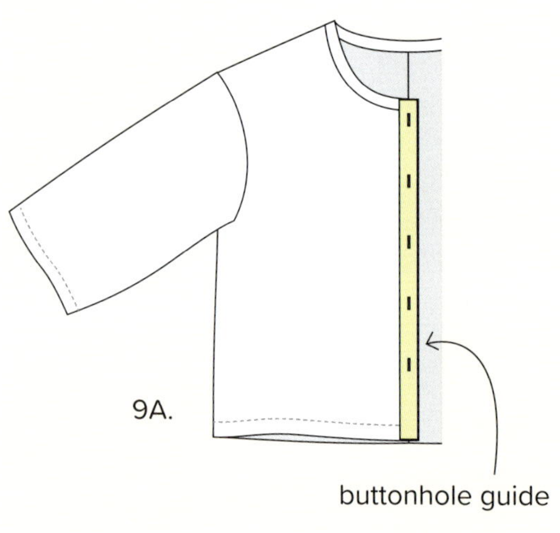

9. Make buttonholes

A. Place buttonhole guide—located with your paper pattern pieces—on right side (as worn). Match top of guide to top edge of neckline. Mark buttonholes with a fabric pen. Sew buttonholes according to your sewing machine instructions.

10. Attach buttons

A. Overlap right button placket over left button placket. Find center of buttonholes and make a mark on left button placket. Sew buttons in place by hand or according to your sewing machine instructions.

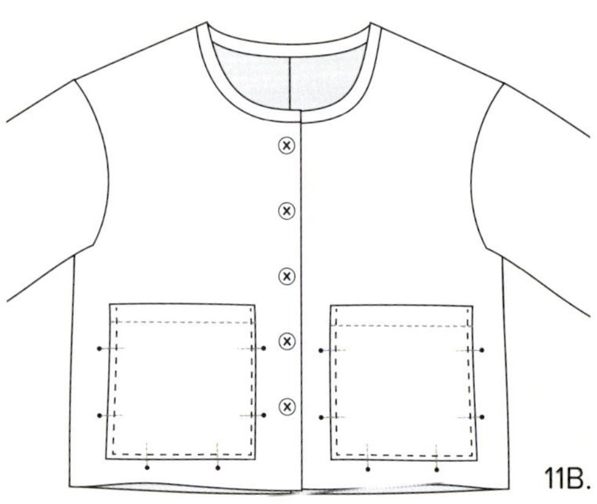

11. Attach pockets (optional)

A. Follow patch pocket assembly method on page 42.

B. Determine where you want your pockets. Pin in place. Edge stitch pockets in place using a ⅛-inch (0.3cm) seam allowance around side and bottom edges.

High five! You made a button-up shirt!

RODEO PANTS

Rodeo Pants make a statement with enough pockets to carry all your hopes and dreams.

Skill level: Confident beginner

Techniques: Elastic channel, patch pockets, inserted pockets

Fabric suggestions: Light to midweight wovens such as linens, cottons, canvas, or denim

Notions: Coordinating thread, 1½-inch (4cm) wide elastic

Shape and Style

A high-rise elastic waist and straight leg with knee panels, adorned with optional pockets.

Fit

A loose fit through the hip and thigh, hitting at the top of the foot.

Construction

Knee panels and pockets galore give this simple silhouette tons of personality.

Design Philosophy

Comfort and utility but make it FUN.

Finished garment measurements (inch/cm)

	XXS	XS	S	M	L	XL
Waist before elastic	37½ (95)	39½ (100)	41½ (106)	43½ (110.5)	46 (117)	49 (125)
Hip	39 (99)	41 (104)	43 (109)	45 (114)	47½ (121)	50½ (128)

	2XL	3XL	4XL	5XL	6XL
Waist before elastic	53 (135)	57 (145)	61 (155)	65 (165)	69 (175)
Hip	54½ (139)	58½ (149)	62½ (159)	66½ (169)	70½ (179)

Total fabric requirements (yard/m)

Extra fabric may be needed to match stripes, plaids, or directional prints.

	Length (yard/m)					
Width	XXS	XS	S	M	L	XL
44in 112cm	3 2.8	3 2.8	3 2.8	3 2.8	3¾ 3.5	3¾ 3.5
54in 137cm	2¾ 2.6	2¾ 2.6	2¾ 2.6	2¾ 2.6	3¼ 3	3¼ 3

Width	2XL	3XL	4XL	5XL	6XL
44in 112cm	3¾ 3.5	3¾ 3.5	4¼ 3.9	4¼ 3.9	4¼ 3.9
54in 137cm	3¼ 3	3¼ 3	4¼ 3.9	4¼ 3.9	4¼ 3.9

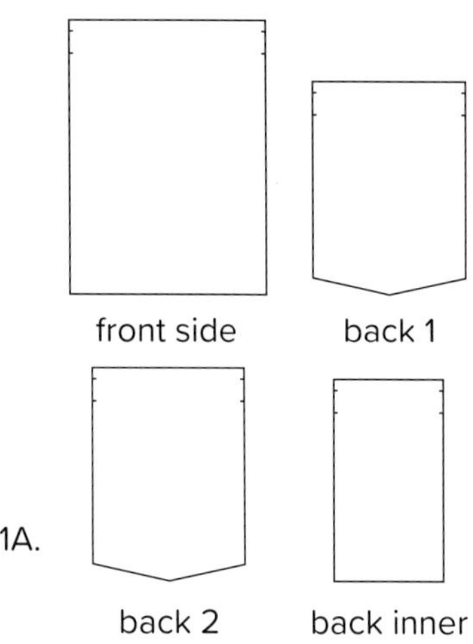

1. Prepare patch pockets

A. Follow instructions for patch pockets on page 42. Use this method for all back pockets and front side patch pocket. Set completed pockets aside to use in steps 4 and 6.

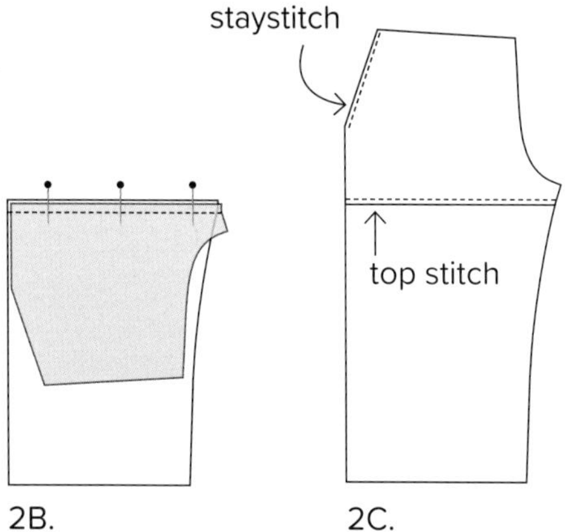

2. Assemble front leg panels

A. To keep its shape, staystitch front diagonal pocket opening on leg.

B. With right sides together align top panel to center panel, matching at notches. Pin in place. Sew with a ½-inch (1.3cm) seam allowance. Finish seam with a zigzag stitch or serger. Press seam toward top panel.

C. Top stitch on top panel using a ¼-inch (0.6cm) seam allowance making sure to catch all seam allowances beneath.

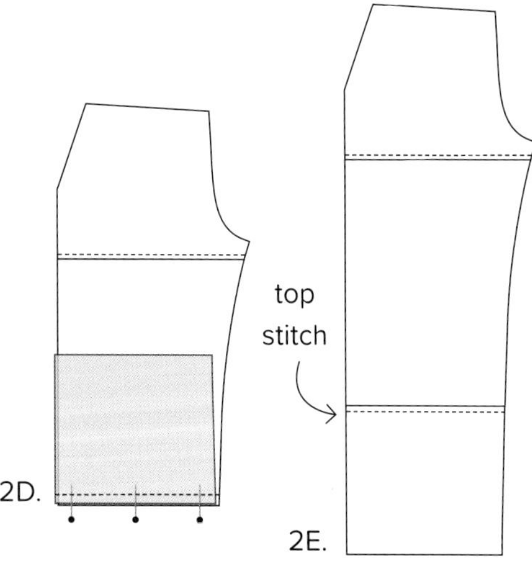

D. With right sides together, align center panel to bottom panel, matching at notches. Pin in place. Sew with a ½-inch (1.3cm) seam allowance. Finish seam with a zigzag stitch or serger. Press seam toward bottom panel.

E. Top stitch on bottom panel using a ¼-inch (0.6cm) seam allowance making sure to catch all seam allowances beneath. Repeat steps 2A–2E for other pant leg.

Piecing lines will not be illustrated in future steps.

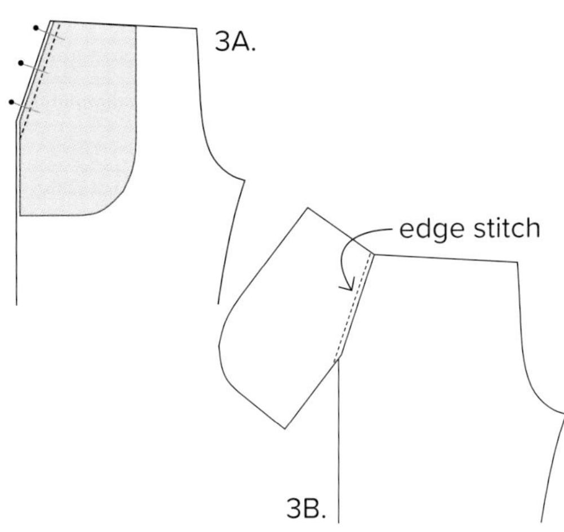

3. Attach front inserted pockets

A. With right sides together, align diagonal side of pocket to diagonal pocket opening on pants. Pin in place. Sew with a ½-inch (1.3cm) seam allowance. Press pocket and seam allowance away from pant leg.

B. Edge stitch pocket opening to seam allowance beneath using a ⅛-inch (0.3cm) seam allowance.

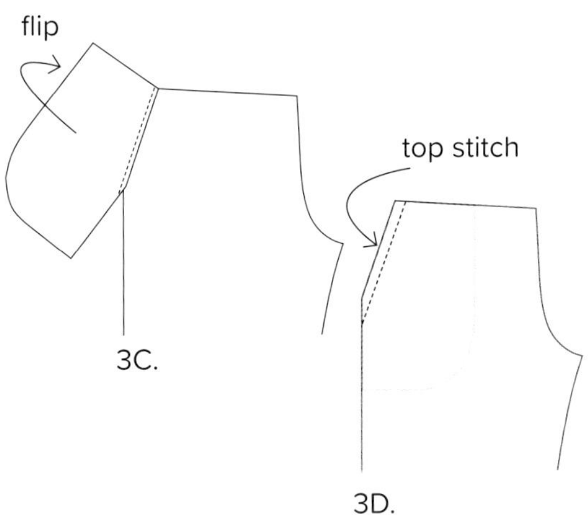

C. Flip pocket toward wrong side of pant leg. The wrong side of pocket will now be touching wrong side of pant leg. Press in place.

D. From right side of garment top stitch along pocket opening using a ¼-inch (0.6cm) seam allowance.

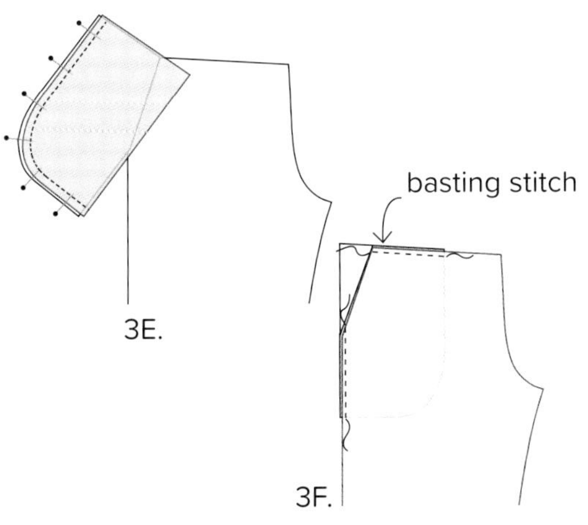

E. Pull pocket away from pant leg. With right sides facing, align pocket bag to pocket. Pin in place. Sew pocket to pocket bag using a ½-inch (1.3cm) seam allowance. Finish seam with a zigzag stitch or serger.

F. Flip completed pocket back toward wrong side of pant leg, matching at notches. Temporarily secure with a basting stitch at top and side of pocket using a ¼-inch (0.6cm) seam allowance. Repeat steps 3A–3F for other inserted pocket.

4. Attach back pockets

A. The small inner pocket can go on either leg. With right sides facing up, use inner pocket placement marks on back leg pattern as a guide to align small inner pocket (made in step 1A) to back pant leg. Pin in place. Edge stitch with a ⅛-inch (0.3cm) seam allowance.

B. With right sides facing up, use outer pocket placement marks on back leg patterns as a guide to align two back pockets (made in step 1A) to back pant legs. Pin in place. Edge stitch with a ⅛-inch (0.3cm) seam allowance. Repeat for other back pocket.

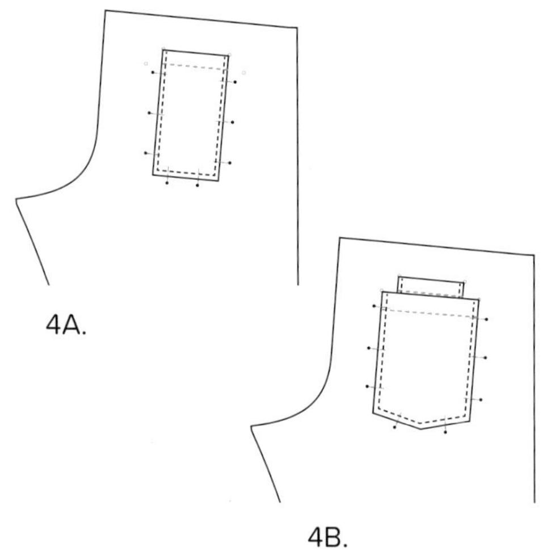
4A.
4B.

5. Sew side seams

A. With right sides together, align side seams. Pin in place. Sew with a ½-inch (1.3cm) seam allowance. Finish seam with a zigzag stitch or serger. Press seam toward back.

B. From right side of garment top stitch on back pant leg using a ¼-inch (0.6cm) seam allowance, making sure to catch all seam allowances beneath. Repeat steps 5A–5B for other leg.

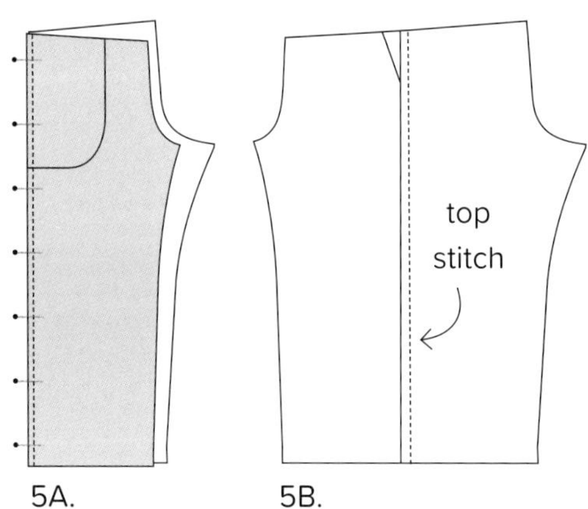

5A.
5B.

6. Attach front side pocket

A. With right sides facing up, use pocket placement mark on front leg pattern as a guide to align front side pocket to front pant leg. Fold front inserted pocket (completed in step 3) out of the way to avoid sewing through it. Pin front side pocket in place, then edge stitch with a ⅛-inch (0.3cm) seam allowance. Have fun with these side pockets—they can be placed wherever you like.

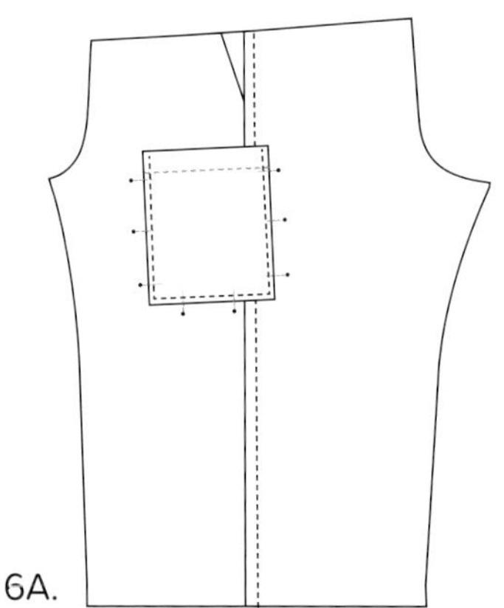
6A.

RODEO PANTS

COLOR STRATEGY

OPPOSITE NEUTRALS

Why it works

This palette uses just two colors—dark denim blue and natural cream—placed on opposite ends of the value scale. The high contrast creates a bold, dynamic look, while the even distribution of each color keeps the overall design balanced and clean.

Tip

Choosing opposites in muted or neutral tones lets you keep the contrast without overwhelming the garment.

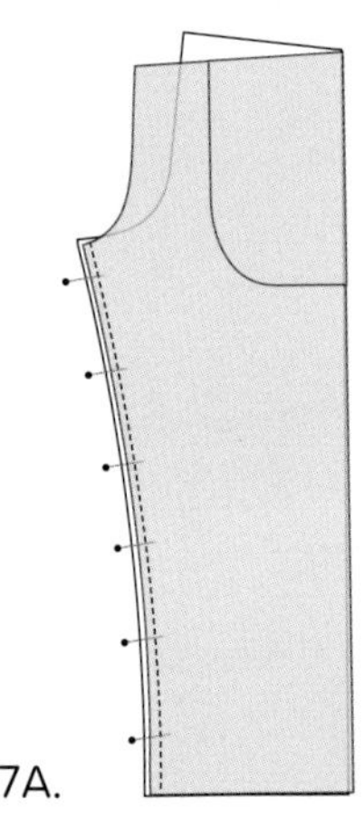
7A.

7. Sew inseams

A. With right sides together, align front and back inseams. Pin in place. Sew with a ½-inch (1.3cm) seam allowance. Finish seam with a zigzag stitch or serger. Press seam toward back. Repeat for other pant leg.

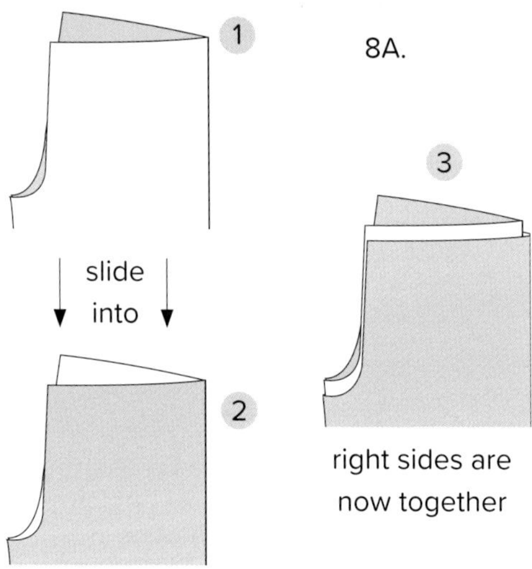

8A.

right sides are now together

8. Connect pant legs

A. Turn one leg inside out while keeping other leg right side out. Slide leg that is right side out into leg that is inside out. The right sides will now be together.

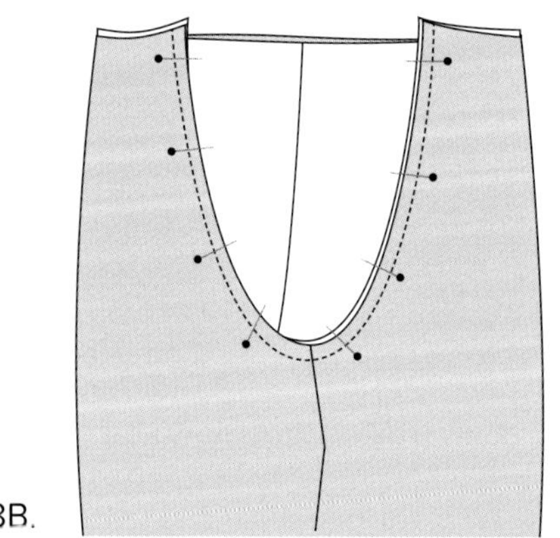
8B.

B. Align front and back rise curves, matching at crotch point. Pin in place. Sew with a ½-inch (1.3cm) seam allowance. Finish with a zigzag stitch or serger. Press seam toward one side.

9. Prepare waistband

9A.

A. With right sides together, match short ends of waistband. Pin in place on either side. Sew with a ½-inch (1.3cm) seam allowance. Press seams open.

B. With wrong sides together, fold waistband in half lengthwise. Press in place.

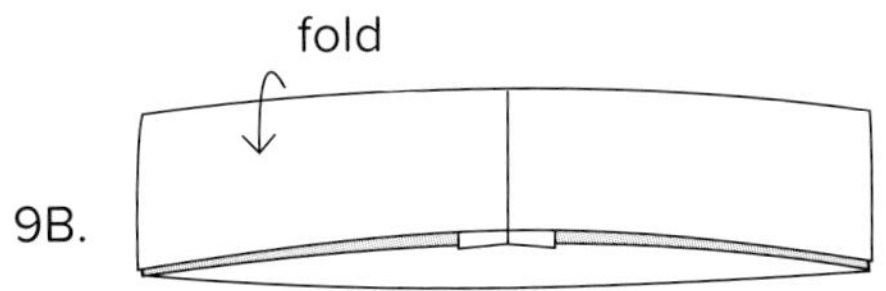

9B.

C. With right sides together, match folded raw edge of waistband to pant opening. Match waistband seams to front and back seams of pants. Pin in place. Sew with a ½-inch (1.3cm) seam allowance, leaving an opening to insert elastic by starting and stopping 1½ inches (4cm) away from center back.

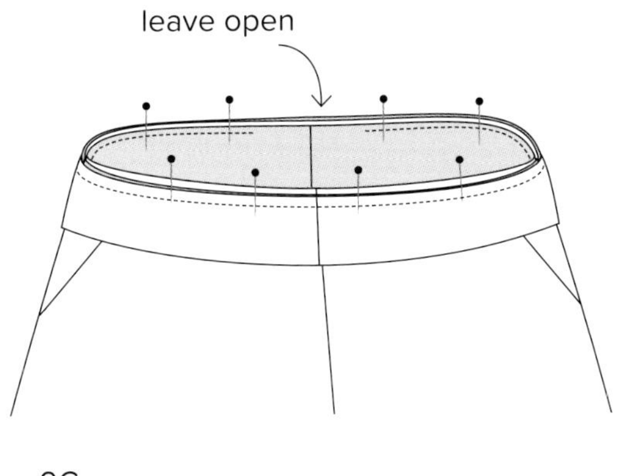

9C.

D. Without stretching it, cut a piece of 1½-inch (4cm) wide elastic to a length that fits comfortably around your waist, plus 1 inch (2.5cm) extra. Attach a safety pin to one end of the elastic and feed through opening of waistband channel, making sure it does not get twisted along the way. When the two elastic ends meet, overlap by 1 inch (2.5cm), pin in place, and sew elastic together forming a rectangle. Backstitch to secure.

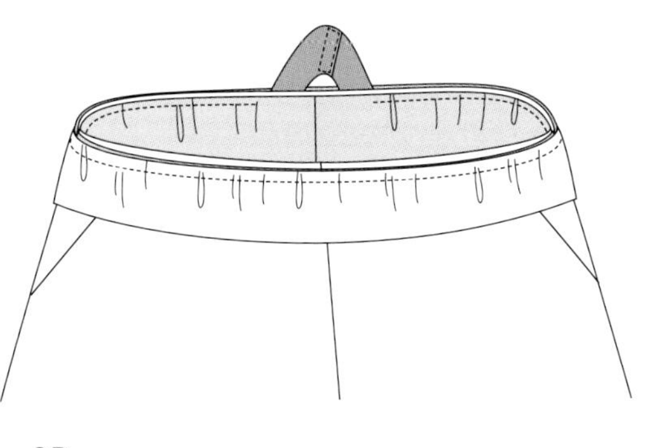

9D.

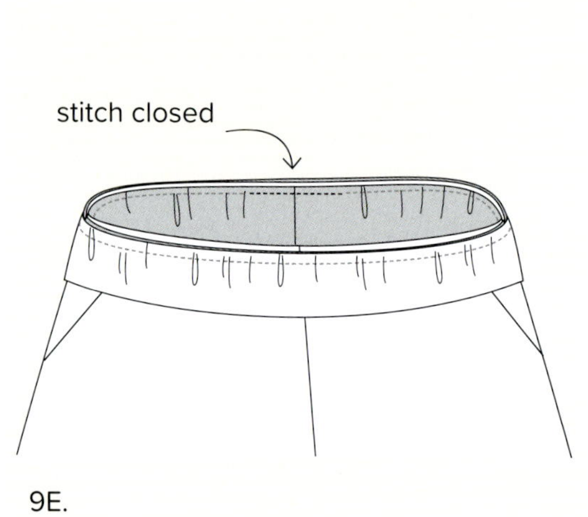

9E.

E. Sew the back waistband opening closed, taking care not to stitch through the elastic. Distribute elastic around channel so the gathering is even. Finish seam with a zigzag stitch or serger. Press seam toward pants.

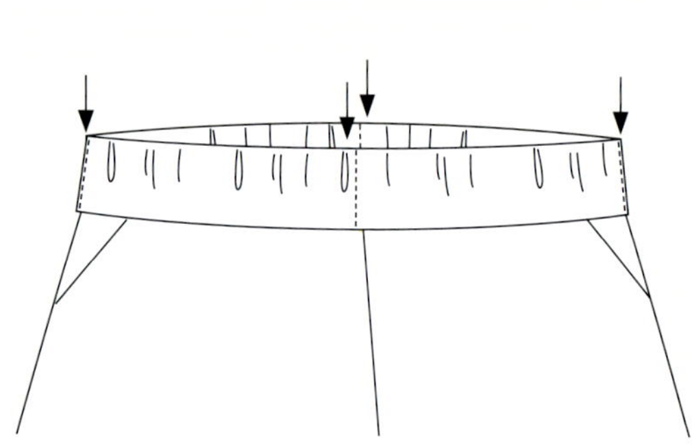
9F.

F. With garment right side out, sew vertical lines through all layers of waistband at center front seam, center back seam, and side seams. This will keep elastic in place during wear and washing.

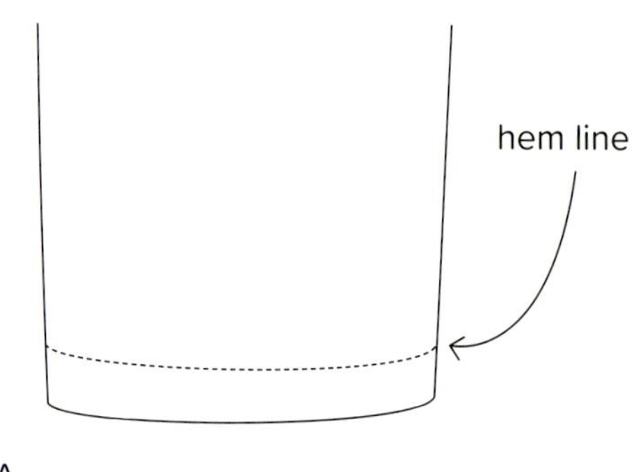

10A.

10. Hem pant legs

A. Press raw edge of pant leg under ½ inch (1.3cm) toward wrong side. Press under again by another 1 inch (2.5cm). Pin in place and sew along top folded line. Repeat for other pant leg.

For details on hemming see page 40.

Yay, pants complete!

GALA DUSTER

The Gala Duster combines everything you've learned to make in a statement layering piece.

Skill level: Confident beginner

Techniques: Sleeves, inseam pockets, ties, collar band

Fabric suggestions: Light to midweight wovens such as linens, cottons, denim

Notions: Coordinating thread

Shape and Style
Smock-like dress with a full gathered skirt, bracelet length sleeves, and a V-neck style front that closes with wide ties at the bodice.

Fit
Loose, with dropped shoulders, and hits below the knee.

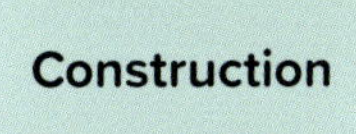

Construction
Fun and easy to sew with maximum patchwork possibilities.

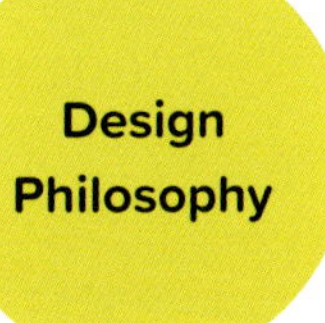

Design Philosophy
Simple shapes and techniques combine to create a dramatic canvas for creative scrap theory play.

Finished garment measurements (inch/cm)

	XXS	XS	S	M	L	XL
Chest	41½ (106)	43½ (110.5)	45½ (115.5)	47½ (121)	50 (127)	53 (135)
Hip/Hem	62 (158)	64 (163)	66 (168)	70 (178)	76 (193)	80 (203)

	2XL	3XL	4XL	5XL	6XL
Chest	57 (145)	61 (155)	65 (165)	69 (175)	73 (185)
Hip/Hem	86 (218)	92 (234)	98 (249)	104 (264)	110 (279)

Total fabric requirements (yard/m) Extra fabric may be needed to match stripes, plaids, or directional prints.

	Length (yard/m)					
Width	XXS	XS	S	M	L	XL
44in 112cm	4 3.7	4 3.7	4 3.7	4 3.7	5½ 5.1	5½ 5.1
54in 137cm	3¼ 3	3¼ 3	3¼ 3	3¼ 3	5¼ 4.9	5¼ 4.9

Width	2XL	3XL	4XL	5XL	6XL
44in 112cm	5½ 5.1	5½ 5.1	5¾ 5.3	5¾ 5.3	5¾ 5.3
54in 137cm	5¼ 4.9	5¼ 4.9	5¾ 5.3	5¾ 5.3	5¾ 5.3

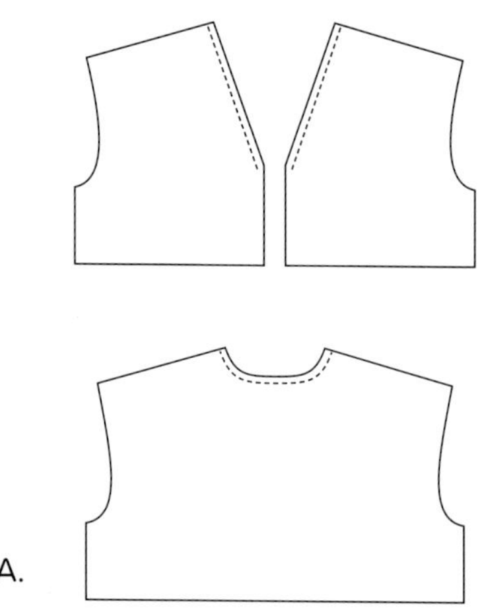

1A.

1. Staystitch

A. Staystitch front and back necklines (refer to page 38 on how to staystitch).

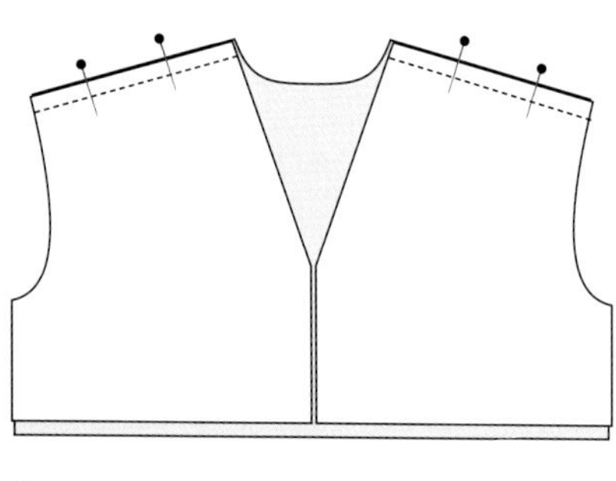

2A.

2. Sew shoulder seams

A. With right sides together, pin front and back shoulders. Sew both shoulders with a ½-inch (1.3cm) seam allowance. Finish seam with a zigzag stitch or serger. Press seams toward back.

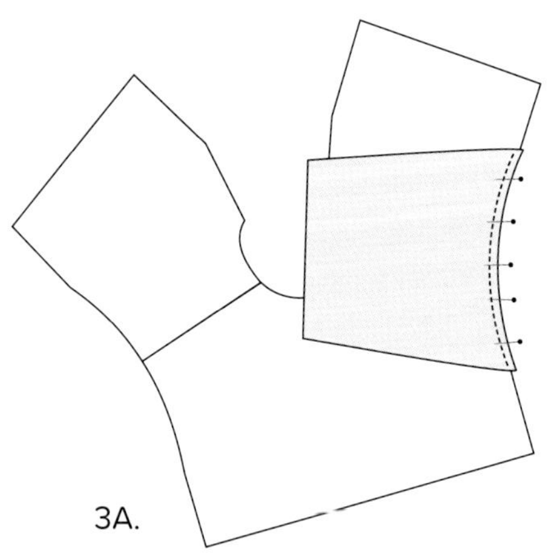

3A.

3. Attach sleeves

A. With right sides together, align sleeve to armhole, matching at notches. The center notch will align with the shoulder seam. Sew with a ½-inch (1.3cm) seam allowance. Finish seam with a zigzag stitch or serger. Press seam toward sleeve. Repeat for other sleeve.

4. Sew side seams

A. With right sides together, match front and back side seams aligning at underarm seam. Sew with a ½-inch (1.3cm) seam allowance. Finish seam with a zigzag stitch or serger. Press seam toward back. Repeat for other side.

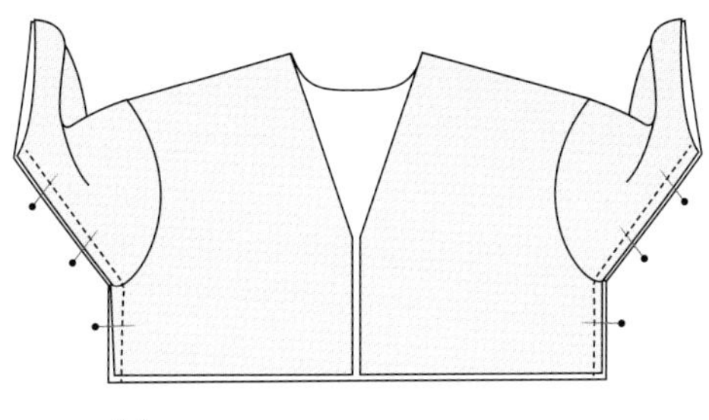

4A.

5. Prepare and attach sleeve cuffs

A. With right sides together, pin short ends of cuff. Sew with a ½-inch (1.3cm) seam allowance, creating a loop. Press seam open.

B. With wrong sides together, fold the cuff in half lengthwise and press.

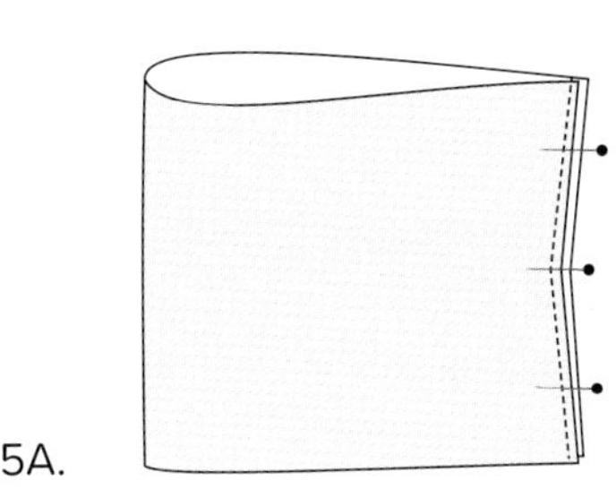

5A.

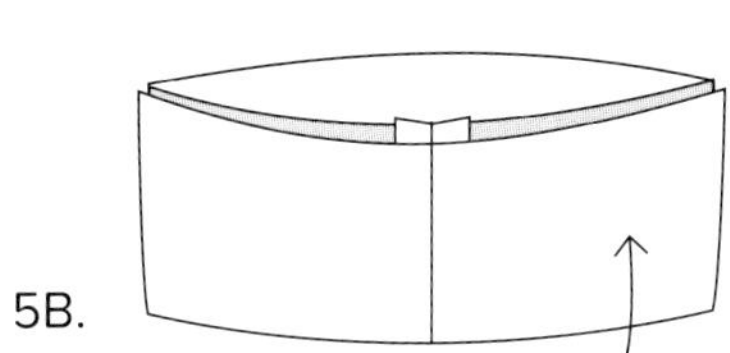

5B.

C. With garment inside out, slide the folded cuff into the sleeve opening, matching the raw edges. Line up the cuff seam to the sleeve seam.

D. Pin in place. Sew with a ½-inch (1.3cm) seam allowance. Finish seam with a zigzag stitch or serger. Press seam toward sleeve. Repeat for other sleeve.

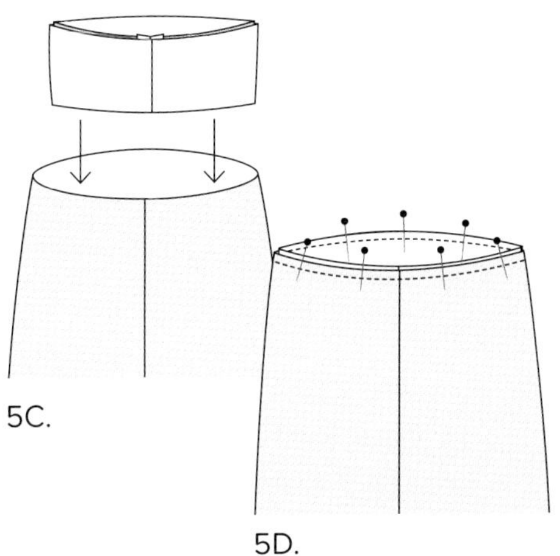

5C.

5D.

Front skirt width x 32 inches (81.3cm) high

	XXS	XS	S	M	L	XL
IN	16	16½	17	18½	19½	20½
CM	40.5	42	43.3	47	49.5	52
	2XL	3XL	4XL	5XL	6XL	
IN	22	23½	25	26½	28	
CM	56	59.8	63.5	67.3	71	

Back skirt width x 32 inches (81.3cm) high

	XXS	XS	S	M	L	XL
IN	32	33	34	37	39	41
CM	81.3	84	86.5	94	99	104
	2XL	3XL	4XL	5XL	6XL	
IN	44	47	50	53	56	
CM	112	119.5	127	134.5	142	

6. Prepare skirt panels

A. Piece together fabric scraps or use a single piece of fabric (some sizes will require piecing). Cut final fabric pieces to meet the measurements in the charts to the left. You will need two pieces of fabric to these measurements for the front skirt and one piece of fabric for the back skirt.

B. To find center point of **back skirt** refer to step 4A from Swing Tank instructions (see page 110). You will not need to find center point of front skirt.

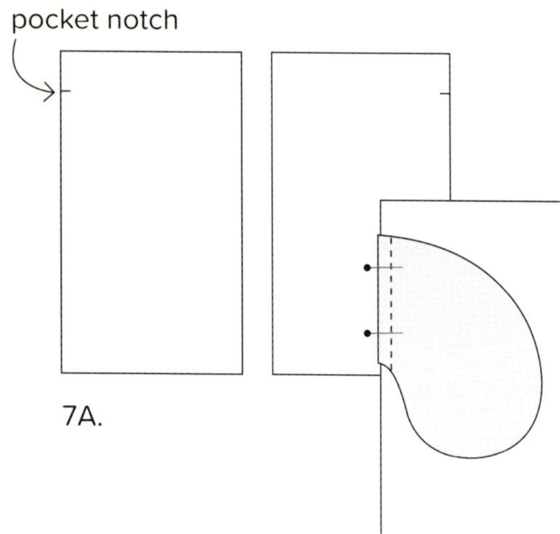

7A.

7. Attach inseam pockets to skirt panels

A. To find pocket notch placement, measure 1 inch (2.5cm) down from top of skirt panel on both side seams for front and back skirt panels. Make a small notch. Continue by following directions for attaching inseam pockets on page 43.

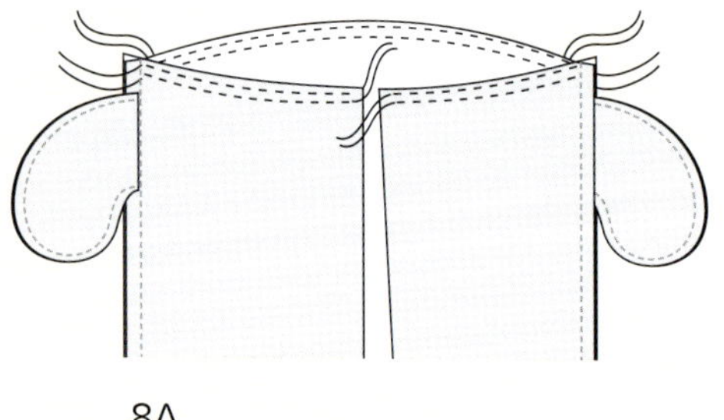
8A.

8. Gather and attach skirt

A. Your front and back skirt panels are now connected with inseam pockets attached. Continue by following instructions on page 39 on how to gather. Gather each front skirt panel starting and stopping just before side seams and 1 inch (2.5cm) before center front. Gather back skirt separately, starting and stopping just before side seams.

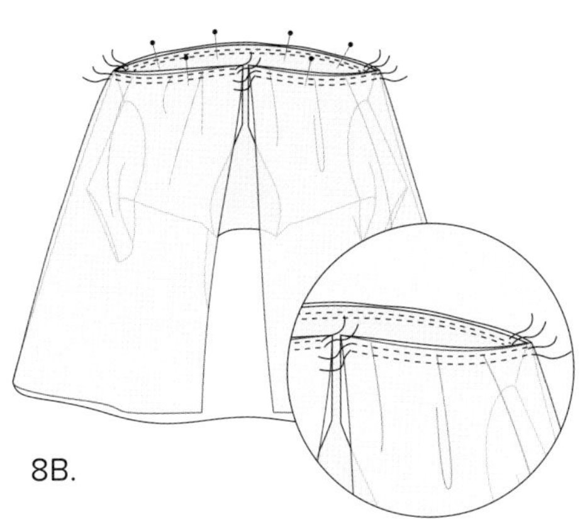

8B.

B. With right sides together, match gathered edge of skirt to bottom edge of body. Align skirt and body at center back notch, side seams, and front openings. Evenly distribute gathers and pin in place. Sew with a ½-inch (1.3cm) seam allowance. Remove visible gathering stitches. Finish seam with a zigzag stitch or serger. Press seam toward body.

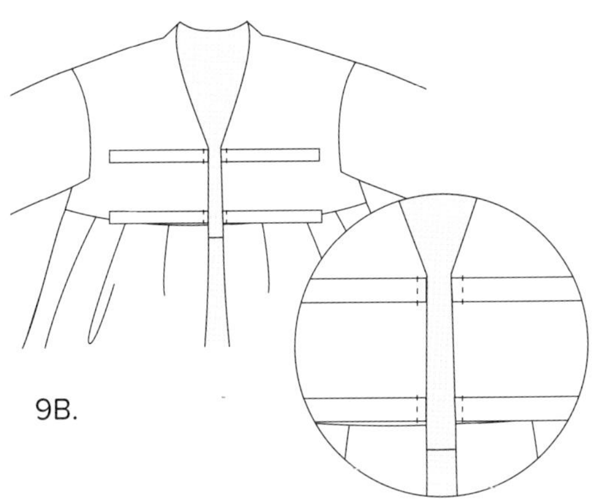

9B.

9. Make and position ties

A. Follow method on page 41 for making ties. You will need four completed ties.

Tie size: 14 x 3 inches (36 x 8cm)

B. With garment right side out, match raw edge of tie to raw edge of body. Place first tie right below front body notch and second tie right above where body and skirt meet. Temporarily attach ties with a basting stitch using a ¼-inch (0.6cm) seam allowance. Repeat on other side of body.

10. Prepare and attach collar band

A. Cut two collar bands according to measurement chart below.

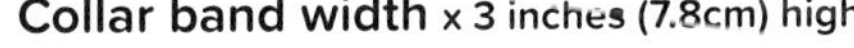

Collar band width x 3 inches (7.8cm) high

	XXS	XS	S	M	L	XL
IN	50	50½	51	51½	52½	53
CM	127	128.3	129.5	131	133.3	134.5
	2XL	**3XL**	**4XL**	**5XL**	**6XL**	
IN	53½	54	54½	56	56½	
CM	136	137	138.5	142	143.5	

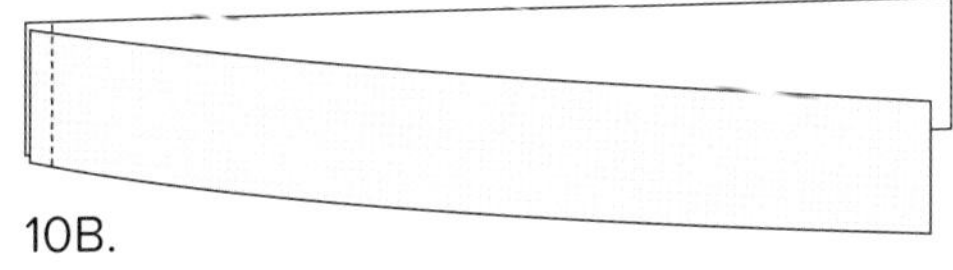

10B.

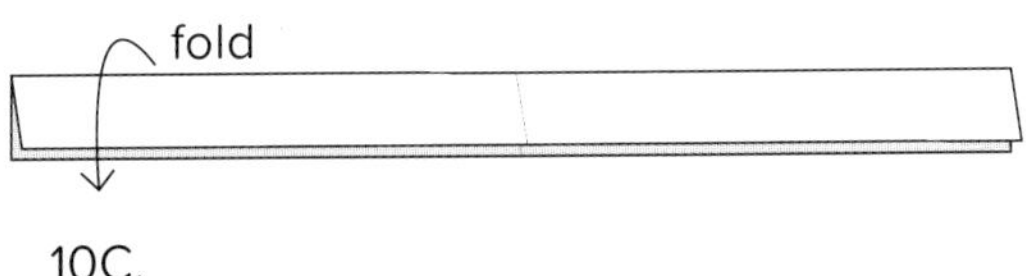

10C.

B. Sew with a ½-inch (1.3cm) seam allowance, creating a long strip. Press seam open.

C. With wrong sides touching fold collar band in half lengthwise. Press.

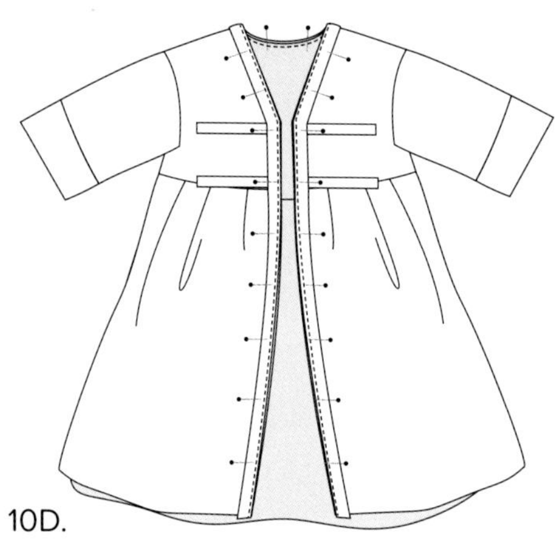

10D.

D. With right sides together, align raw edge of folded collar band to front opening of garment. Match collar band seam to center back notch of body (this is the center of back neckline). Starting from center back, continue to align and pin the collar band to the garment until you reach the hem. Your ties will be sandwiched between the collar band and body. Sew with a ½-inch (1.3cm) seam allowance. Finish seam with a zigzag stitch or serger. Fold the collar band over and press seam toward the body.

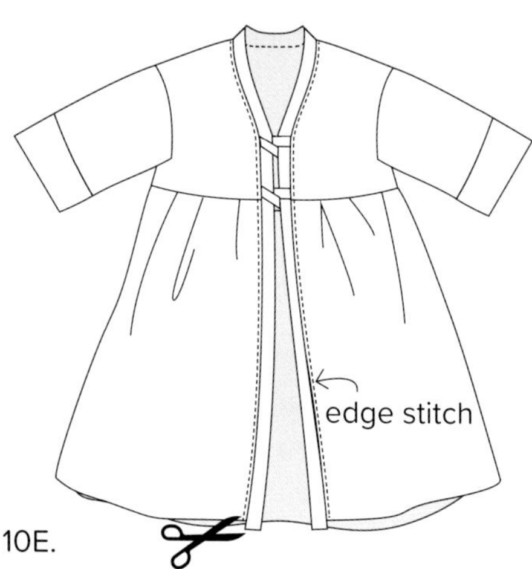

10E.

E. With ties folded out of the way, edge stitch on the body side around entire collar band with a minimal seam allowance, making sure to catch all the seam allowances beneath. Trim off any excess collar band that extends past the skirt length.

11A.

11. Hem skirt

A. To hem the skirt, press the raw edge of skirt hem under by ½ inch (1.3cm) toward wrong side. Press under again by another 1½ inches (4cm). Pin in place and sew along folded line.

For details on hemming see page 40.

GALA DUSTER

COLOR STRATEGY

ULTRA SCRAPPY NEUTRALS

Why it works

Choosing a neutral palette with a range of light to dark values creates a sense of harmony, with no single color overpowering the rest. This is a simple way for your patchwork to feel intentional and stylish rather than chaotic.

Tip

When patchworking, choose fabric scraps with a similar surface area—even if they're different shapes. This maintains visual balance and makes piecing your project easier and more harmonious.

PILLOWCASE TOTE

The Pillowcase Tote is a slim, quilted tote with short handles and a mini ruffle edge for ultimate cuteness.

Shape and Style
Slender with rounded bottom corners, adorned with major statement mini ruffles.

Fit
Perfect size for a laptop, notebook, and your latest read.

Construction
A fully lined and quilted project that comes together quickly.

Design Philosophy
Functional and cute.

Skill level: Confident beginner

Techniques: Quilting, gathering, lining

Fabric suggestions: Light to midweight wovens such as linens, cottons, twill, denim, or canvas

Batting: Lightweight cotton batting. We use the brand "Warm & Natural" cotton batting

Notions: Coordinating thread, fusible interfacing (optional)

Finished measurements (inch/cm)

12 x 14 inches (30.5 x 35.5cm) width x height

Total fabric requirements (inch/cm) Extra fabric may be needed to match stripes, plaids, or directional prints.

Fabric	W x H	Total Qty
Main	14 x 16 (35.5 x 40.5)	cut 2
Lining	13 x 14½ (33 x 37)	cut 2
Batting	14 x 16 (35.5 x 40.5)	cut 2
Ruffle	31 x 2½ (79 x 6.4)	cut 2
Handles	15 x 3 (38 x 7.8)	cut 2

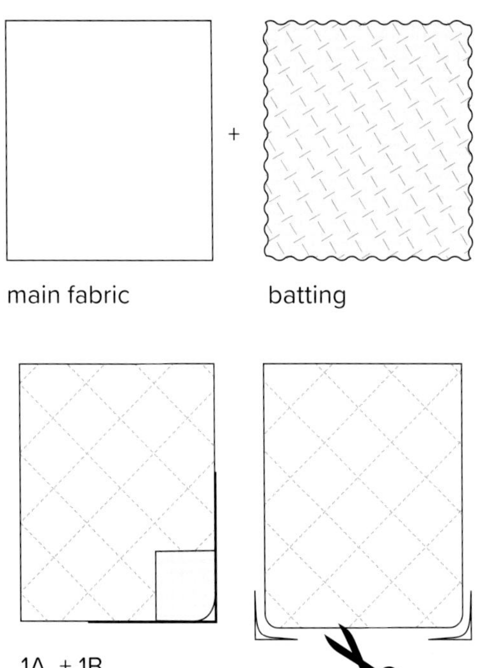

1. Quilt exterior panels

A. Cut two main fabric and two batting fabric according to the measurements in the measurement chart. Follow quilting instructions on page 44 to quilt the main fabric to the batting. Cut newly quilted pieces to be 13-inch (33cm) width x 15-inch (38cm) height. We will now refer to these panels as "exterior front panel" and "exterior back panel."

B. Use the rounded corner template as a guide to cut both bottom corners of both front and back exterior panels.

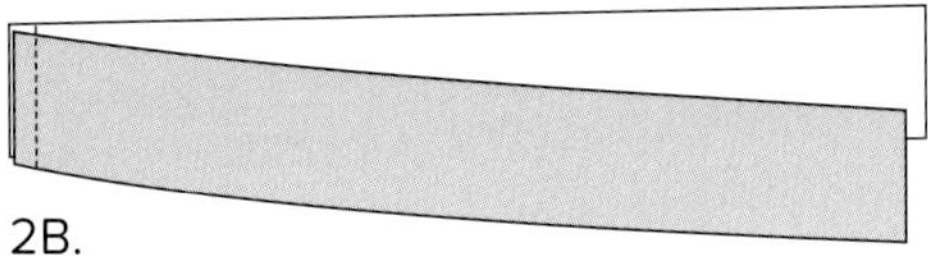

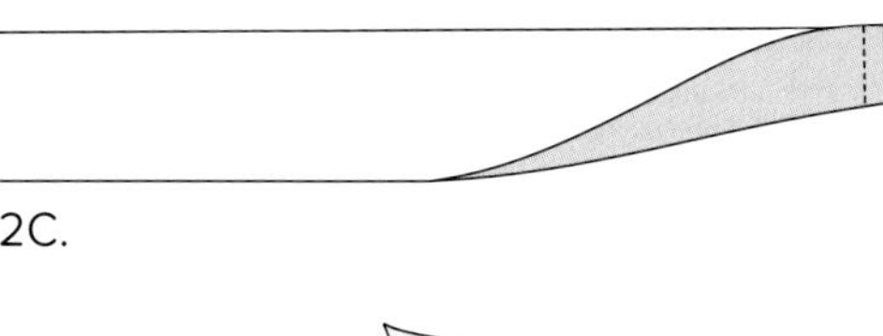

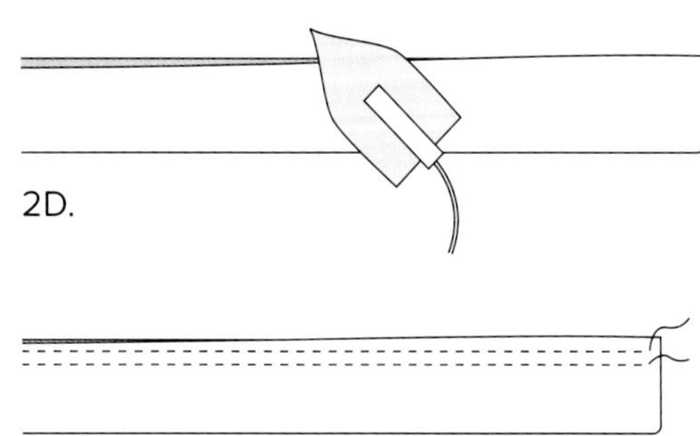

2. Prepare ruffle

A. Cut ruffle pieces according to the measurements in the measurement chart.

B. With right sides together, match one of the short ends from the two ruffle pieces. Sew with a ½-inch (1.3cm) seam allowance. Press seam open, forming a long strip.

C. With right sides together fold the short ends in half. Sew with a ½-inch (1.3cm) seam allowance on both short ends.

D. Flip ruffle so that right side faces out. Use a long sharp object, such as a knitting needle, to push out the corner to a point. Press in half along entire strip. Raw ends on short ends are now enclosed.

E. With ruffle still folded, follow the gathering instructions on page 39 to gather the raw edges of folded ruffle.

3. Attach ruffle

A. From top edge of the front exterior panel measure down ⅝ inch (1.5cm) on both sides. Make a mark on both sides.

B. With right side of the front exterior panel facing up, align gathered edge of ruffle to sides and bottom of panel. Match ruffle's center to bottom center of panel, and start and stop at marks made in Step 3A. Distribute gathers evenly. Pin in place. Temporarily hold ruffle in place by sewing a basting stitch using a ¼-inch (0.6cm) seam allowance.

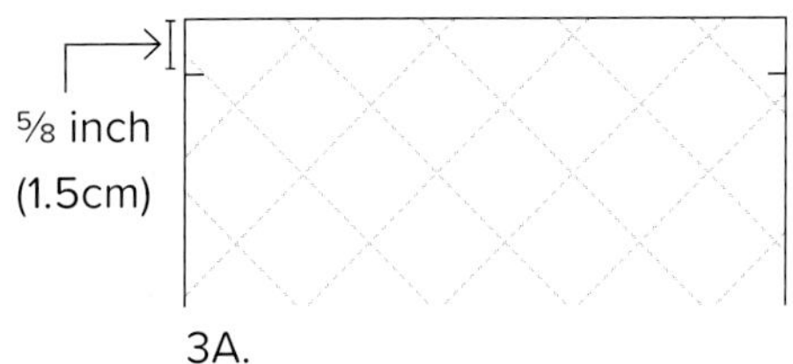

3A.

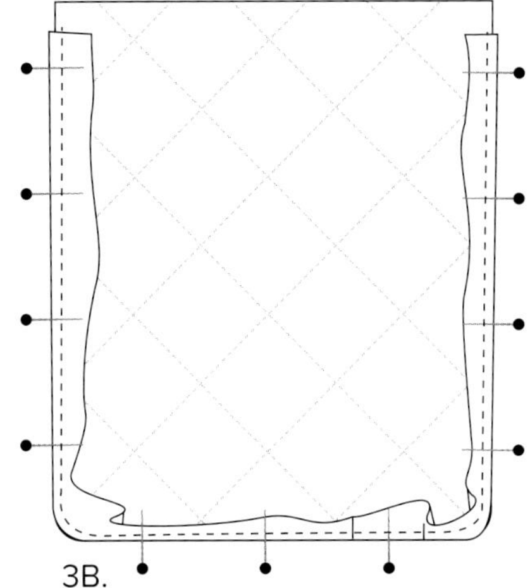

3B.

4. Prepare handles

A. To add stability to handles you can apply fusible interfacing to wrong side of the handle fabric. To apply to fabric, follow directions from the fusible interfacing you are using.

B. With wrong sides together, fold handle in half lengthwise. Press in place to form a crease. Open back out.

C. Fold top and bottom edges toward wrong side to meet center crease. Press in place.

D. Fold in half along the center crease. Press in place.

E. Edge stitch with a minimal seam allowance along long open end. Repeat all steps for other handle.

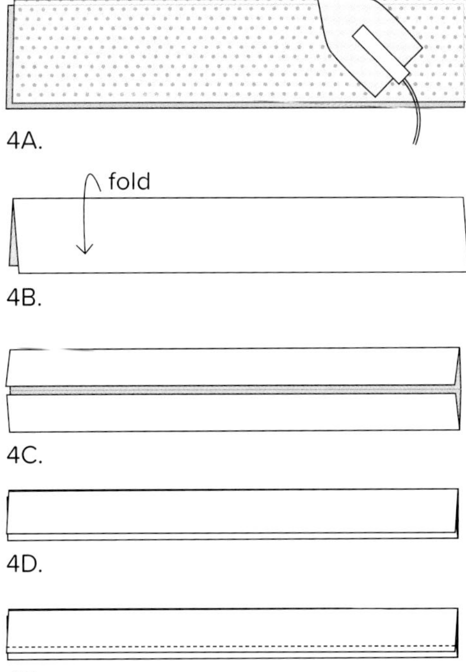

4A.

4B.

4C.

4D.

4E.

5. Attach handles

Ruffle not shown. Be aware it has been attached in step 3B.

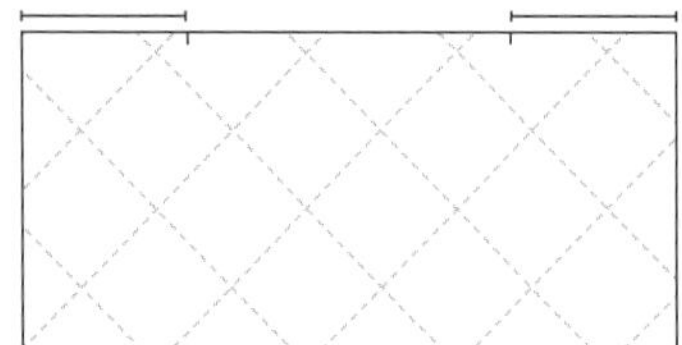

5A.

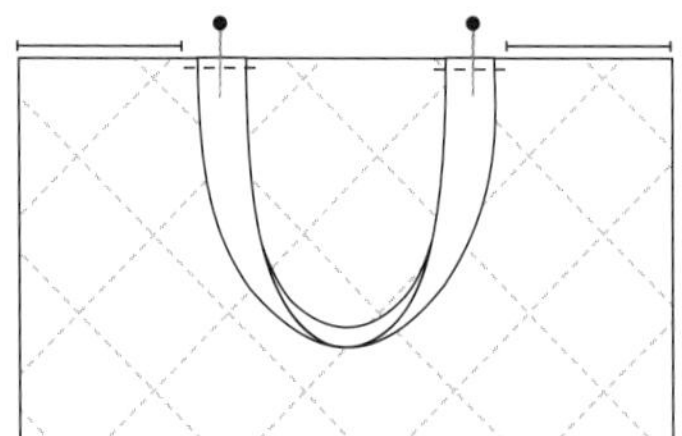
5B.

A. From top edge of front exterior panel measure 3½ inches (9cm) toward the center on either side. Make a mark. Repeat for exterior back panel.

B. With exterior front panel right side facing up, align either end of handle so that the outer edge of handle meets the 3½-inch (9cm) mark. Be careful not to twist the handle. Temporarily secure by basting handles using a ¼-inch (0.6cm) seam allowance. Repeat for remaining handle and exterior back panel.

6. Assemble exterior tote

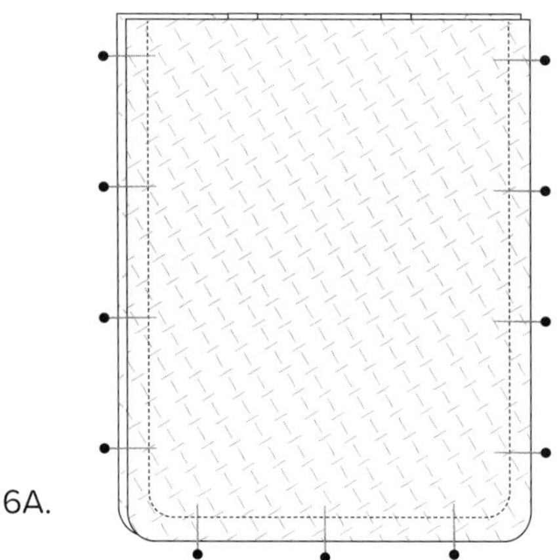
6A.

A. With right sides together, pin front and back exterior panels at both sides and bottom. The ruffle will be sandwiched between the front and back panels and the handles will be facing down. Sew with a ½-inch (1.3cm) seam allowance.

7. Prepare lining

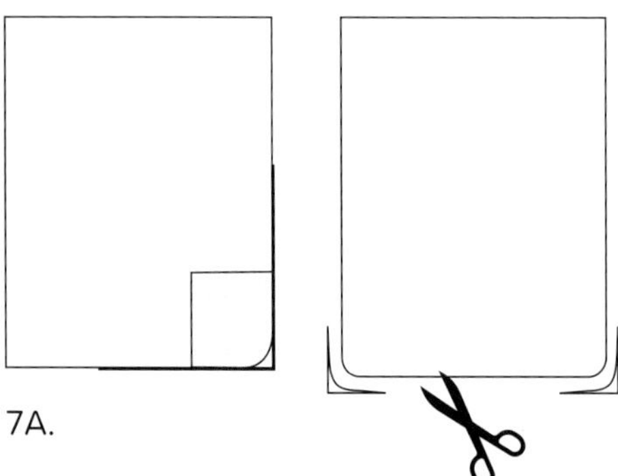
7A.

A. Use the rounded corner template as a guide to cut both bottom corners of both front and back lining panels.

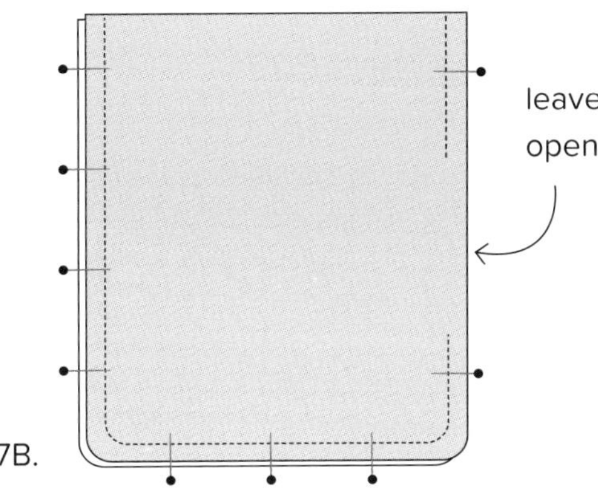

7B.

B. With right sides together, pin front and back lining panels at both sides and bottom. Sew with a ½-inch (1.3cm) seam allowance, leaving a 4-inch (10cm) opening. You will use this opening to turn your tote right side out in a later step.

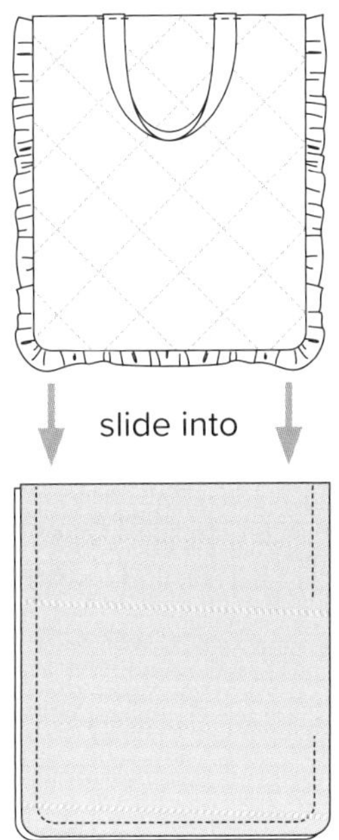

8A.

8. Attach lining to tote

A. With tote right side out and lining still inside out, slide the tote into the lining. Keep the handles facing down. The right side of the tote will now be touching the right side of the lining.

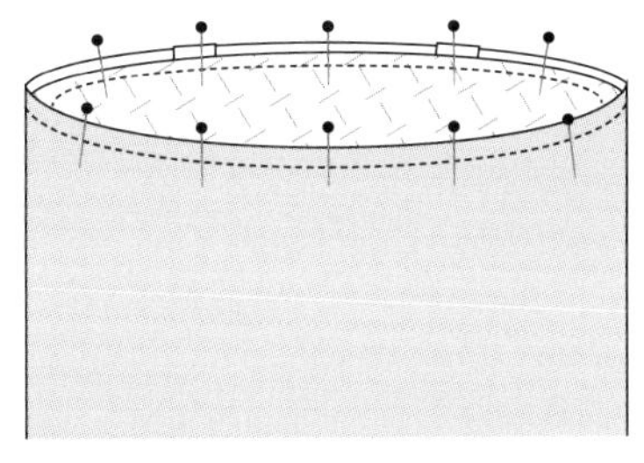
8B.

B. Align at side seams and pin around upper raw edge. Sew with a ½-inch (1.3cm) seam allowance around entire top edge, going through all layers. The ruffle will sit beneath the stitch line, however, be careful not to catch any parts of the ruffle's outer edge when sewing.

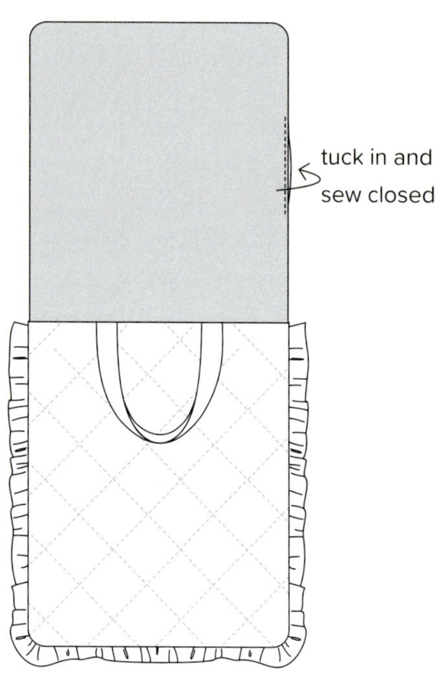

8C.

C. Flip the tote to the right side using the opening made in step 7B. Tuck in the raw edges from opening using the ½-inch (1.3cm) seam allowance as a guide. Pin opening closed and sew shut using a minimal seam allowance.

9. Finish tote

A. Tuck lining toward inside of tote, remove any visible basting stitches, and pull handles up. Neaten, press, and use!

9A.

MATCHY
MATCHY

SWING TANK

The Swing Tank is a peplum-style tank with simple pattern pieces that introduces you to essential sewing techniques.

Skill level: Confident beginner

Techniques: Gathering, bias binding

Fabric suggestions: Lightweight wovens such as linens or cottons

Notions: Coordinating thread

Shape and Style

Flowy and loose. Wear back to front for a whole new look!

Fit

Relaxed with gentle gathered neckline, slim straps, and playful peplum. Hits above hip.

Construction

Learn skill building techniques with minimal pattern pieces.

Design Philosophy

More is more—use any smaller scraps to stretch your color and design creativity.

Finished garment measurements **(inch/cm)**

	XXS	XS	S	M	L	XL
Chest	46 (117)	48 (122)	50 (127)	52 (132)	54½ (139)	57½ (146)
Hip/ Hem	85 (216)	87 (221)	89 (226)	91 (231)	93½ (238)	96½ (245)

	2XL	3XL	4XL	5XL	6XL
Chest	61½ (156)	65½ (166)	69½ (177)	73½ (187)	77½ (196)
Hip/ Hem	100 (254)	103½ (263)	107 (272)	110½ (281)	114 (290)

Total fabric requirements **(yard/m)** Extra fabric may be needed to match stripes, plaids, or directional prints.

	Length (yard/m)					
Width	XXS	XS	S	M	L	XL
44in 112cm	1½ 1.4	1½ 1.4	1½ 1.4	1½ 1.4	1¾ 1.6	1¾ 1.6
54in 137cm	1½ 1.4	1½ 1.4	1½ 1.4	1½ 1.4	1¾ 1.6	1¾ 1.6

Width	2XL	3XL	4XL	5XL	6XL
44in 112cm	1¾ 1.6	1¾ 1.6	2 1.9	2 1.9	2 1.9
54in 137cm	1¾ 1.6	1¾ 1.6	2 1.9	2 1.9	2 1.9

1. Prepare bodice

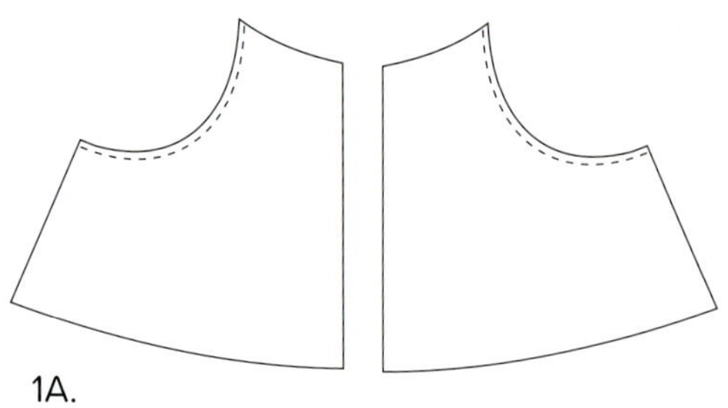

1A.

A. Staystitch armholes (refer to page 38 on how to staystitch).

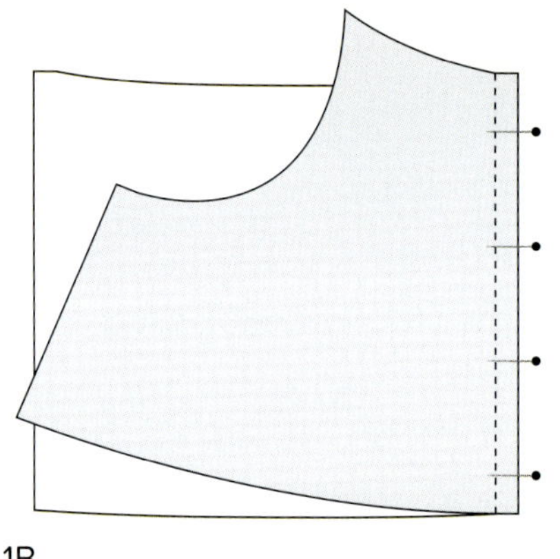

1B.

B. With right sides together, align side panel to center panel. Pin in place. Sew with a ½-inch (1.3cm) seam allowance. Finish seam with a zigzag stitch or serger. Press seam toward side panel. Repeat for other side panel.

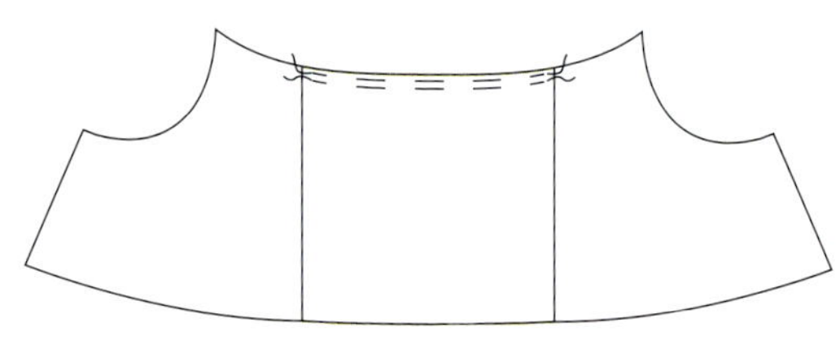

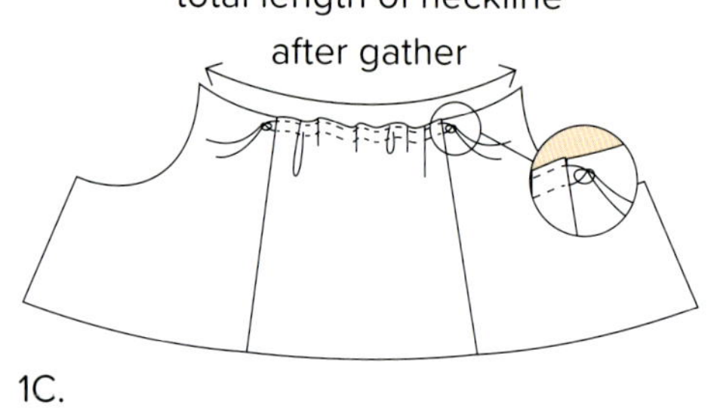

1C.

C. Gather center panel of neckline (refer to page 39 on how to gather). Gather until the total length of neckline meets the measurement in the chart below. To secure measurement in place tie off the ends of gathering threads. Repeat all steps for back bodice.

Total length of neckline

	XXS	XS	S	M	L	XL
IN	10⅜	10¾	11	11¼	11⅝	11⅞
CM	26.5	27.3	28	28.5	29.5	30.3

	2XL	3XL	4XL	5XL	6XL
IN	12¼	12½	12¾	13	13¼
CM	31	31.8	32.4	33	33.8

SWING TANK

Tip

When using several colors, try adding a neutral like black or cream—it gives your eye a place to rest and helps everything feel balanced.

COLOR STRATEGY

MULTI ANALOGOUS

Why it works

Level up your patchwork game with multiple colors and prints. Analogous colors naturally blend because they sit close together on the color wheel, so it's a great strategy to use when selecting several different fabrics. The result is a harmonious, almost rainbow-like effect that feels exciting yet easy on the eyes.

2A.

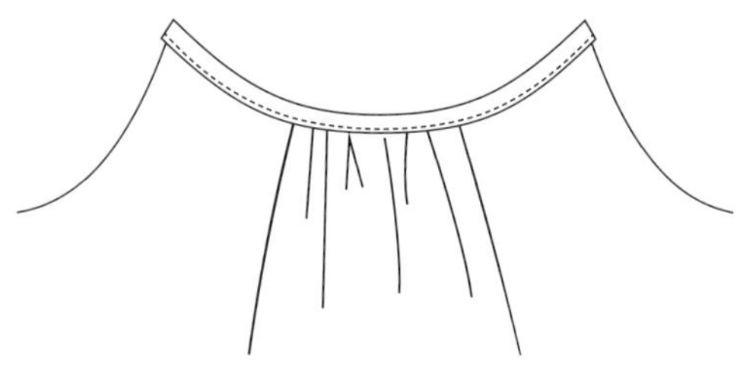

2. Attach neckline bias binding

A. Cut two strips of bias binding to be 1 inch (2.5cm) longer than the total length of neckline. Follow open end bias binding method on page 32 to attach bias binding to neckline. Trim off any extra binding and remove any visible gathering stitches. Do this for both front and back body.

3. Cut peplum

A. Piece together fabric scraps or use a single piece of fabric. Cut final fabric piece to meet the measurement in the chart below. You will need two pieces of fabric this size.

Peplum width x 8 inches (20.5cm) high

	XXS	XS	S	M	L	XL
IN	43½	44½	45½	46½	47¾	49¼
CM	110.5	113	115.5	118	121.3	125
	2XL	3XL	4XL	5XL	6XL	
IN	51	52¾	54½	56¼	58	
CM	129.5	134	138.5	143	147	

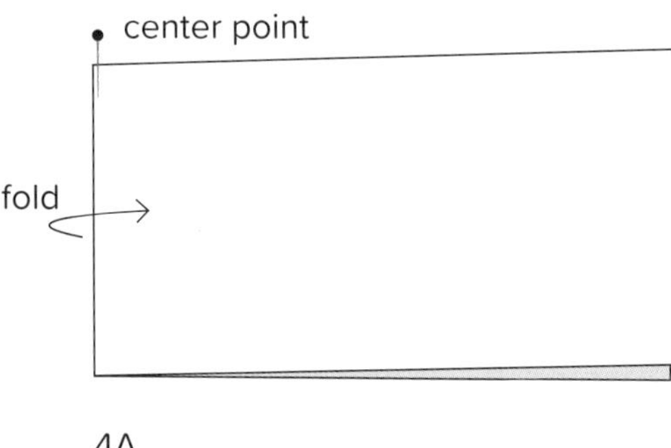

4A.

4. Prepare and attach peplum

A. Find center point of front peplum by folding fabric in half lengthwise. Mark center point with a pin or small notch and ensure center point is facing up. Open peplum. Repeat for back peplum piece.

B. Follow gathering method on page 39 to gather front and back peplum. You will have one gathered panel for the front and one for the back.

C. With right sides together, align gathered edge of front peplum to bottom edge of front bodice, matching at center notch. Distribute gathers evenly as you pin in place. Sew with a ½-inch (1.3cm) seam allowance, with gather side up to keep gathers neat. Finish with a zigzag stitch or serger. Press seam toward body. Repeat for back bodice.

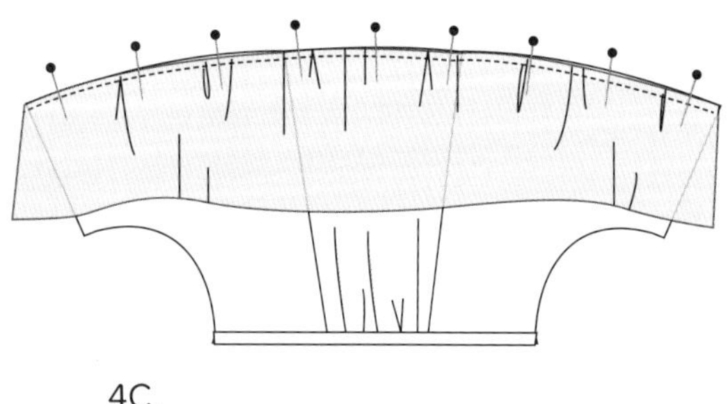

4C.

SWING TANK

COLOR STRATEGY

FUN MONOCHROMATIC

Why it works

Red and pink make a striking monochromatic pair because they share the same base hue—red—but sit at different points on the value and saturation scale. The boldness of red is softened by the addition of pinks.

Tip

Using a bold color in a monochromatic palette a great way to make a statement that's both cheerful and polished.

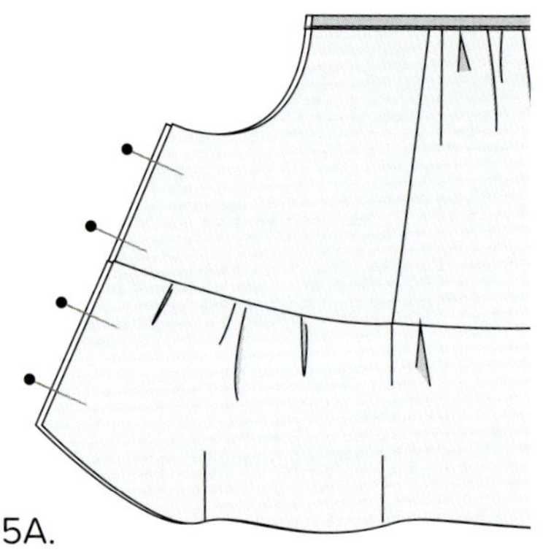
5A.

5. Sew side seams

A. With right sides together, align front and back side seams. Pin in place. Sew with a ½-inch (1.3cm) seam allowance. Finish with a zigzag stitch or serger. Press seam toward back. Repeat for other side seam.

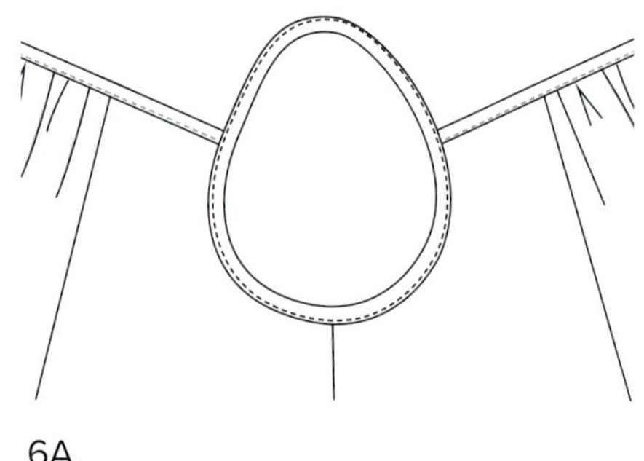
6A.

6. Attach armhole bias binding

A. Cut two lengths of bias according to measurement chart below. Continue by following closed loop bias binding method on page 36. Repeat for both armholes.

Armhole bias length x 1⅝ inches (4cm) high

	XXS	XS	S	M	L	XL
IN	19	20¼	21½	22¾	24¼	26
CM	48.3	51.5	54.5	57.8	61.5	66

	2XL	3XL	4XL	5XL	6XL
IN	28	30¼	32½	34½	36¾
CM	71	77	82.5	87.5	93.3

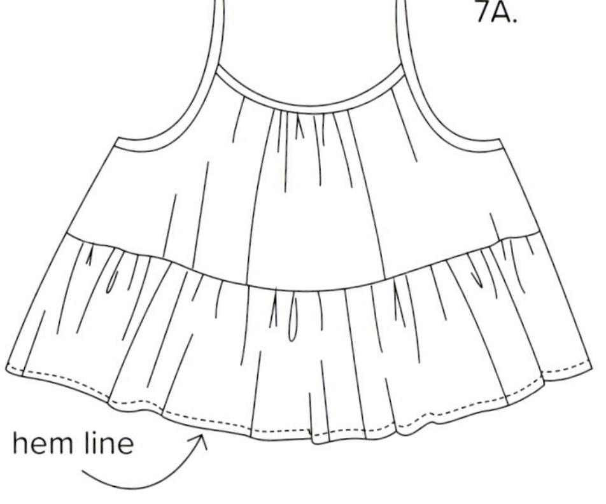

7A.

7. Hem bottom

A. Press raw edge of hem under by ¼ inch (0.6cm) toward wrong side. Press under again by another ¼ inch (0.6cm). Pin in place and sew along folded line.

For details on hemming see page 40.

GALLERY SHIRT

The Gallery Shirt is an effortless and cute top that is deceptively simple. Perfection tied in a bow!

Skill level: Confident beginner

Techniques: Sleeves, ties, bias binding with tails, gathering

Fabric suggestions: Lightweight wovens such as linens or cottons

Notions: Coordinating thread

Shape and Style
Roomy with two front ties, short sleeves, and short gathered peplum.

Fit
Relaxed with dropped shoulders and hits at the natural waist.

Construction
Fun to sew pre-divided panels for pattern and color creativity.

Design Philosophy
Bow closures add a sweet little flair to this versatile top.

Finished garment measurements (inch/cm)

	XXS	XS	S	M	L	XL
Chest	41½ (106)	43½ (110.5)	45½ (115.5)	47½ (121)	50 (127)	53 (135)
Hip/ Hem	65 (165)	68 (173)	71 (180)	74 (188)	78 (198)	82 (208)

	2XL	3XL	4XL	5XL	6XL
Chest	57 (145)	61 (155)	65 (165)	69 (175)	73 (185)
Hip/ Hem	88 (224)	94 (239)	100 (254)	106 (269)	112 (285)

Total fabric requirements (yard/m) Extra fabric may be needed to match stripes, plaids, or directional prints.

	Length (yard/m)					
Width	XXS	XS	S	M	L	XL
44in 112cm	1¾ 1.6	1¾ 1.6	1¾ 1.6	1¾ 1.6	2½ 2.3	2½ 2.3
54in 137cm	1½ 1.4	1½ 1.4	1½ 1.4	1½ 1.4	2 1.9	2 1.9

Width	2XL	3XL	4XL	5XL	6XL
44in 112cm	2½ 2.3	2½ 2.3	2½ 2.3	2½ 2.3	2½ 2.3
54in 137cm	2 1.9	2 1.9	2½ 2.3	2½ 2.3	2½ 2.3

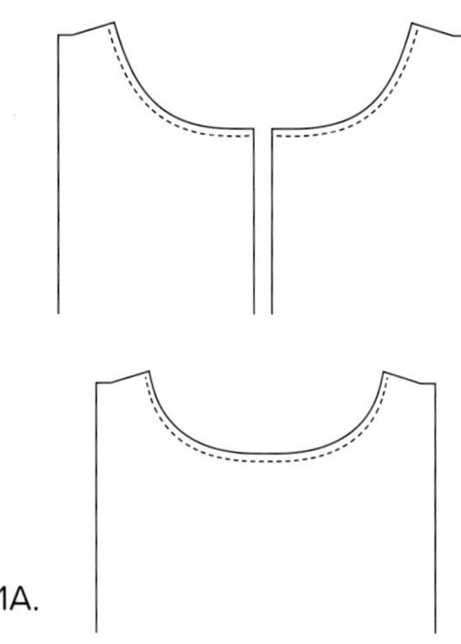

1. Staystitch

A. Staystitch front and back necklines (refer to page 38 on how to staystitch).

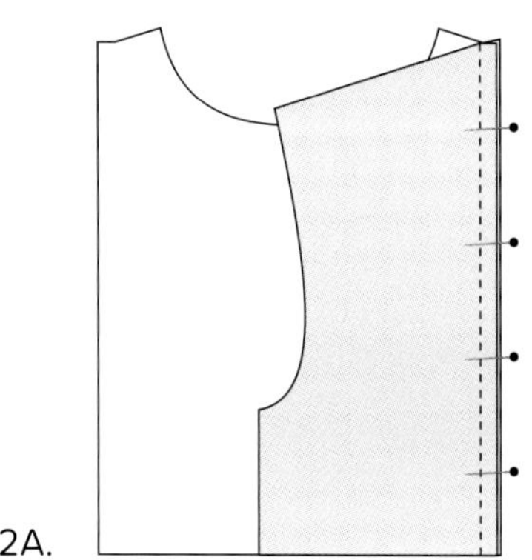

2. Piece back body

A. With right sides together, pin back side panel to back center panel. Sew with a ½-inch (1.3cm) seam allowance. Finish with a zigzag stitch or serger. Press seam toward side panel. Repeat for other side panel. You now have a completed back body.

Completed back body

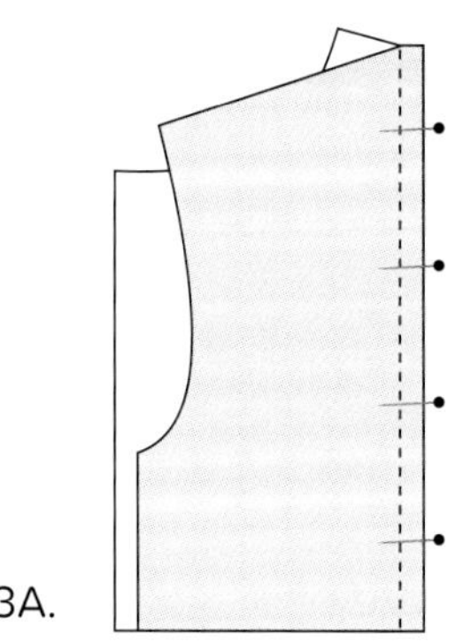

3. Piece front body

A. With right sides together, pin front side panel to front center panel. Sew with a ½-inch (1.3cm) seam allowance. Finish seam with a zigzag stitch or serger. Press seam toward side panel. Repeat for other side.

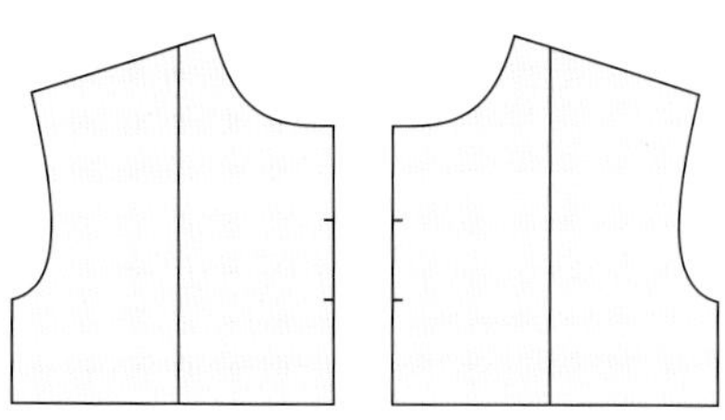

Completed front panels

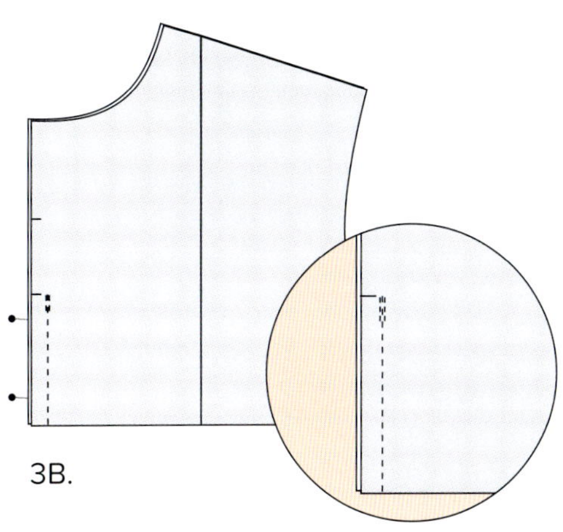
3B.

B. With right sides together, align completed front panels at center front matching at notches. Pin in place below bottom notch to hem. Sew with a ¾-inch (2cm) seam allowance starting from bottom notch to hem. For extra security, backstitch several times at notch.

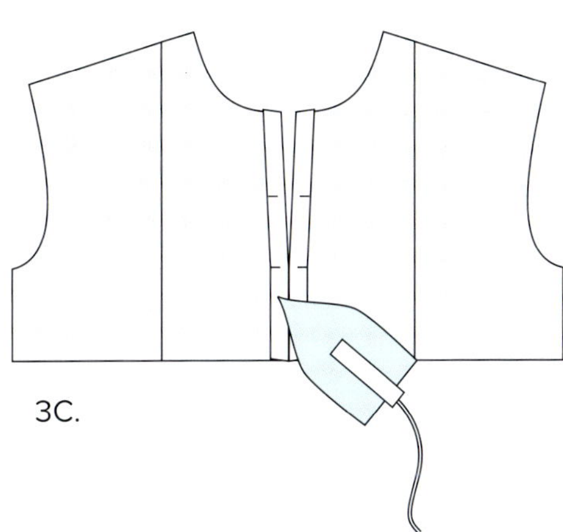
3C.

C. Press seam open continuing all the way up to the neckline using the same ¾-inch (2cm) seam allowance as a guide.

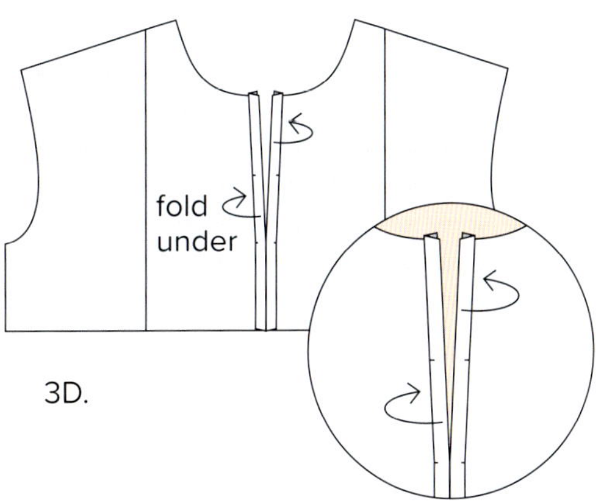

3D.

D. Fold seam allowance under so that the raw edge lines up with the stitch line made in step 3B. The raw edge of the seam allowance will now be hidden. Press in place.

4. Make and attach ties

A. Follow method on page 41 for making ties. You will need two completed ties.

Tie size: 14 x 1⅝in (36 x 4cm)

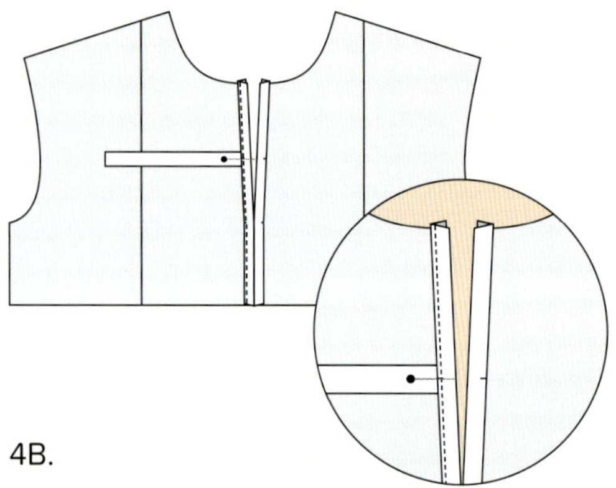

4B.

B. Center tie with the top notch, tuck raw edge of tie under the folded seam allowance. Pin in place. Edge stitch on folded edge from neckline to hem, sewing through the tie.

4C.

C. Fold tie back on itself so that it is facing toward the open slit. Pin in place.

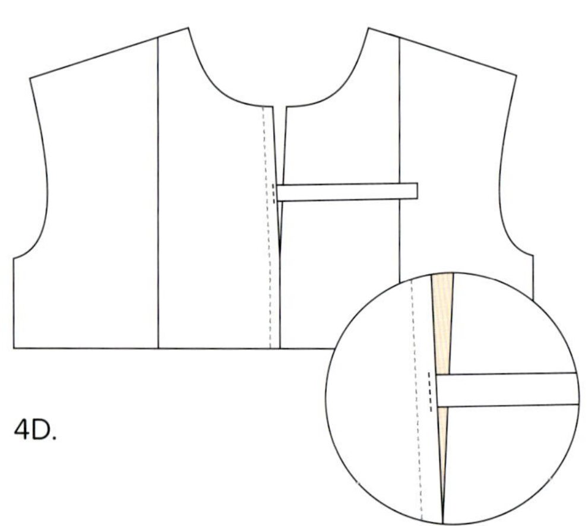

4D.

D. From right side of garment, secure the tie by sewing a small stitch line where the tie meets the body. Repeat steps 4B–4D for the other tie.

COLOR STRATEGY

CLASSIC MONOCHROMATIC

GALLERY SHIRT

Tip

Start with one color and one type of print—like gingham in varying scales—to ease into patchwork without feeling overwhelmed.

Why it works

Black and natural is a timeless monochromatic combo—classic, elegant, and effortlessly stylish. Using gingham in three different scales adds visual interest and depth while keeping things cohesive and simple.

5. Attach shoulder seams

A. With right sides together, pin front and back shoulders. Sew with a ½-inch (1.3cm) seam allowance. Finish seam with a zigzag stitch or serger. Press seams toward back.

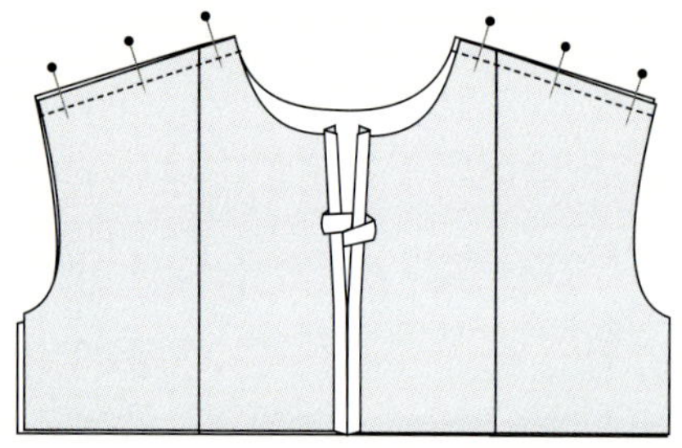

5A.

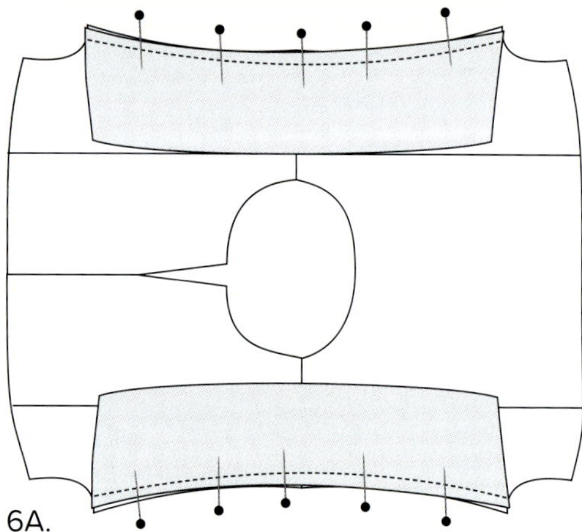

6A.

6. Attach sleeves

A. With right sides together, align sleeve to armhole, matching at notches. The center notch will align with shoulder seam. Sew with a ½-inch (1.3cm) seam allowance. Finish seam with a zigzag stitch or serger. Press seam toward sleeve. Repeat for other sleeve.

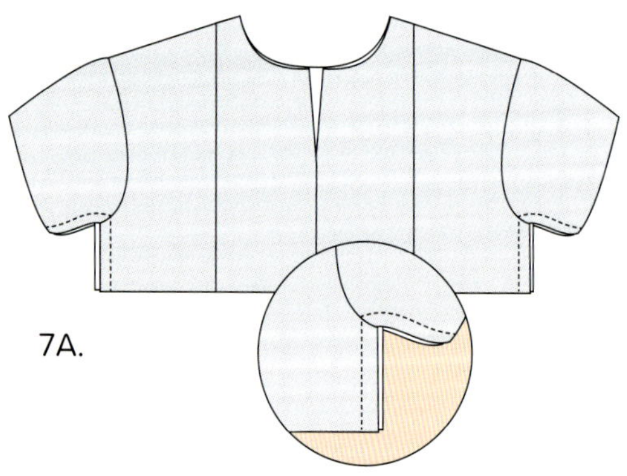

7A.

7. Sew side seams

A. With right sides together, match front and back side seams, aligning at underarm seam. Sew with a ½-inch (1.3cm) seam allowance. Finish seam with a zigzag stitch or serger. Press seam toward back. Repeat for other side.

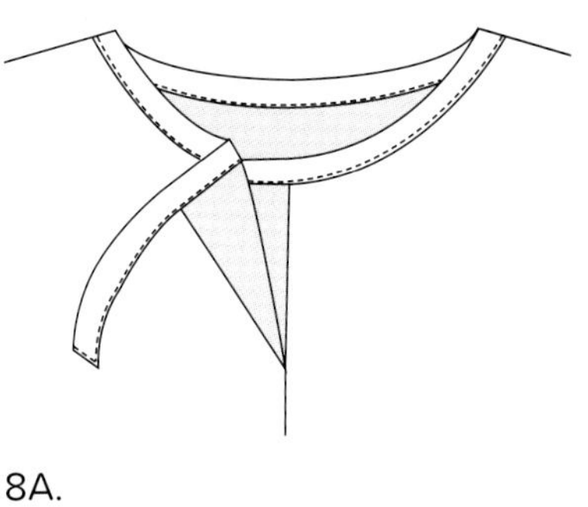

8A.

8. Attach neckline bias binding

A. Cut one length of bias according to the measurement chart below. Continue by following the bias binding with tails method on page 34.

Neckline bias length x 1⅝ inches (4cm) high

	XXS	XS	S	M	L	XL
IN	47½	48½	49¼	50	50¾	51½
CM	120.7	123.3	125	127	129	131
	2XL	**3XL**	**4XL**	**5XL**	**6XL**	
IN	52¼	53	53¾	54½	55¼	
CM	132.7	134.5	136.5	138.5	140.3	

Peplum width x 9 inches (23cm) high

	XXS	XS	S	M	L	XL
IN	33½	35	36½	38	40	42
CM	85	89	92.8	96.5	101.5	106.7
	2XL	**3XL**	**4XL**	**5XL**	**6XL**	
IN	45	48	51	54	57	
CM	114	122	129.5	137	145	

9. Prepare peplum

A. Piece together fabric scraps or use a single piece of fabric. Cut final fabric piece to meet the measurement in the chart to the left. You will need two pieces of fabric this size.

B. To find center point of peplum refer to step 4A from Swing Tank instructions (see page 110).

10. Attach peplum

A. With right sides together, pin front and back peplum pieces at side seams. Make sure the center mark you just made faces up. Sew with a ½-inch (1.3cm) seam allowance creating a large loop. Finish seams with a zigzag stitch or serger. Press seams toward back.

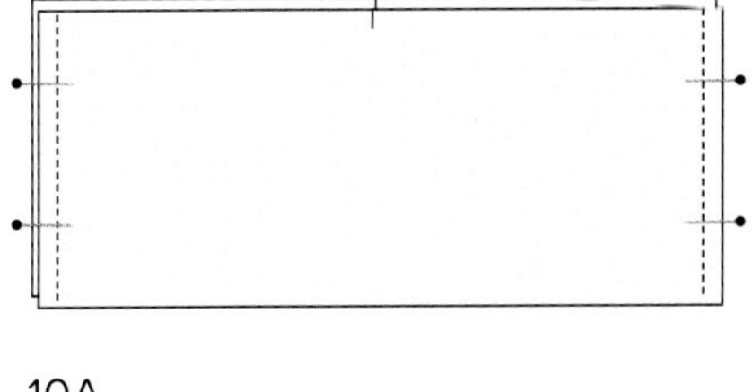

10A.

B. Gather front peplum and back peplum separately, starting and stopping just before the side seams. Follow instructions on page 39 on how to gather.

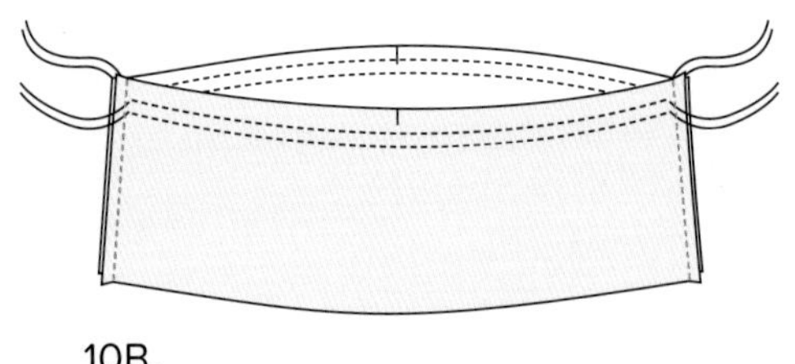

10B.

C. With right sides together, align gathered edge of peplum to bottom edge of body, matching at center notches and side seams. Evenly distribute gathers and pin in place. Sew with a ½-inch (1.3cm) seam allowance. Remove visible gathering stitches. Finish seam with a zigzag stitch or serger. Press seam toward body.

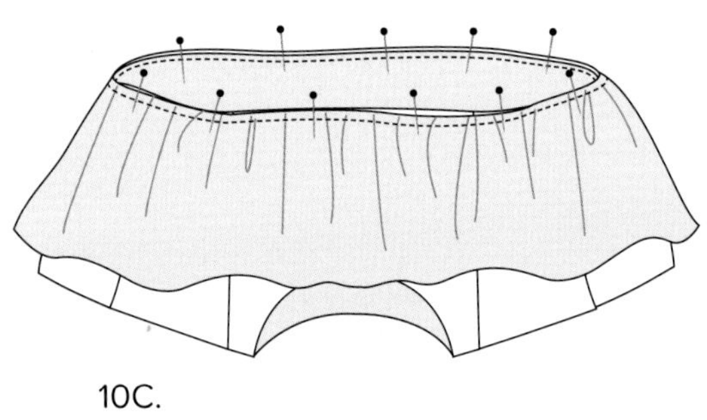

10C.

11. Hem sleeves and body

A. To hem the sleeves, press the raw edge of sleeve hem under by ½ inch (1.3cm) toward wrong side. Press under again by another ½ inch (1.3cm). Pin in place and sew along folded line.

B. To hem the body, press the bottom raw edge under by ½ inch (1.3cm) toward the wrong side. Press under again by another ½ inch (1.3cm). Pin in place and sew along folded line.

For details on hemming see page 40.

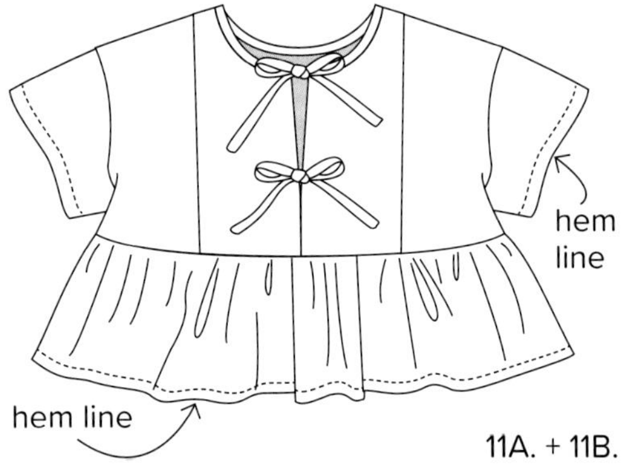

11A. + 11B.

TIE HAT

The Tie Hat is a soft quilted hat with eye-catching wide ties, making it a unique and fashionable accessory.

Shape and Style

Classic bucket shape with medium width brim and chunky side ties.

Fit

Slouchy fit with a flexible brim.

Construction

Fully lined and reversible.

Design Philosophy

Cool, quirky, and shaded.

Skill level: Confident beginner

Techniques: Quilting, easing in shapes

Fabric suggestions: Light to midweight wovens such as cottons, linens, twill, denim, or canvas

Batting: Lightweight cotton batting. We use the brand "Warm & Natural" cotton batting

Notions: Coordinating thread

Finished garment measurements (inch/cm)

24 inches (61cm) circumference

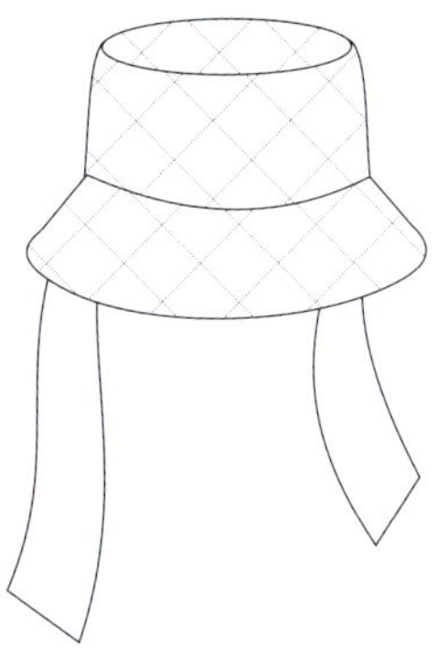

Total fabric requirements (inch/cm) Extra fabric may be needed to match stripes, plaids, or directional prints.

Fabric	W x H	Total Qty
Main	40 x 13 (101.5 x 33)	cut 1
Lining	40 x 13 (101.5 x 33)	cut 1
Batting	40 x 13 (101.5 x 33)	cut 1
Ties	6½ x 30 (16.5 x 76)	cut 2

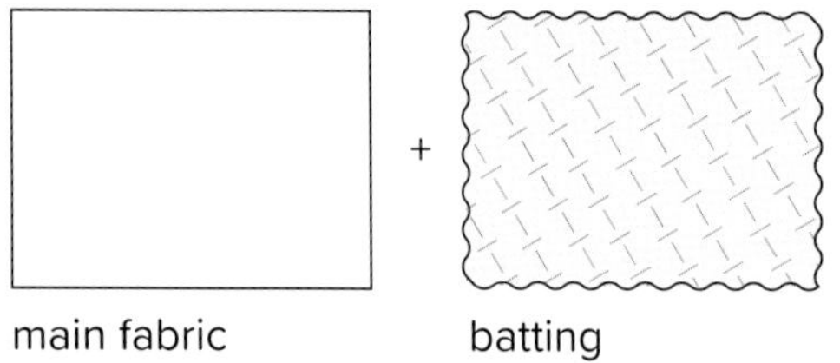

1. Quilt exterior panels

A. Cut one main fabric and one batting fabric according to the measurements in the measurement chart. Follow quilting instructions on page 44 to quilt the main fabric to the batting and cut out one hat top, two crown, and two brim pattern pieces following the cutting diagram to the left. We will now refer to these pattern pieces as "exterior" pattern pieces.

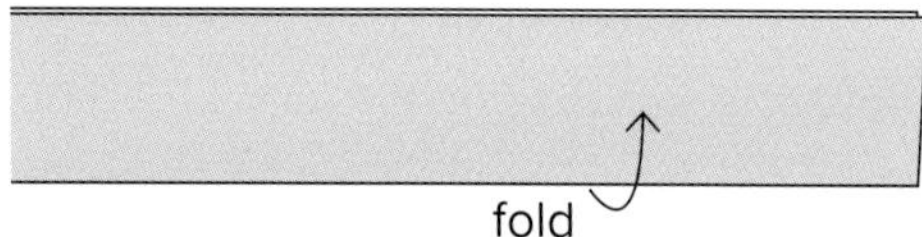

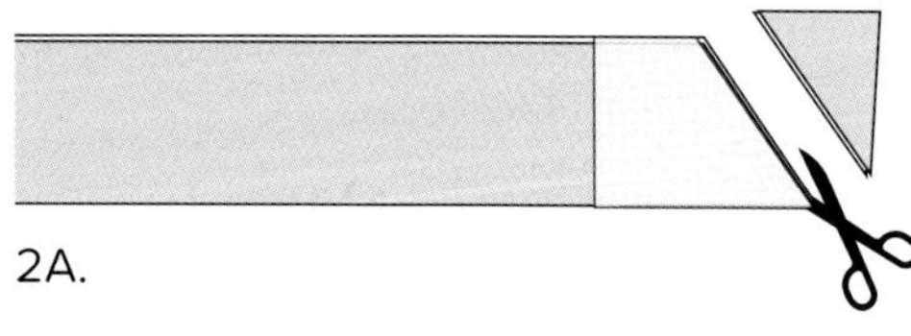

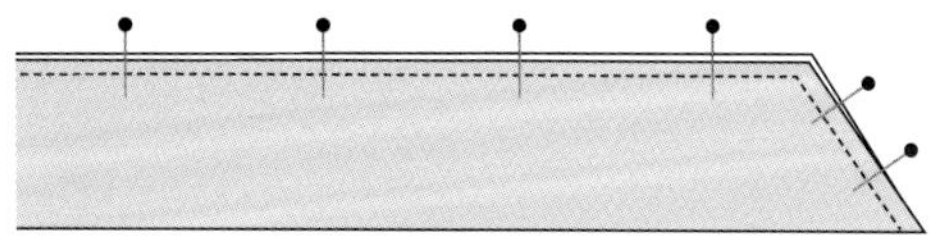

2. Prepare ties

A. With right sides together, fold tie in half lengthwise. Cut one end of the tie at a diagonal using the tie tail template as a guide. The other end will remain square.

B. Pin in place. Sew with a ¼-inch (0.6cm) seam allowance along the long edge and diagonal end. Other short end will remain open for turning.

C. From the open end, flip tie right side out. Use a long sharp object such as a knitting needle to push out the corners to a sharp point. Repeat steps 2A–2C for other tie. Your ties are now complete. Set aside to use in a later step.

3. Cut lining pattern pieces

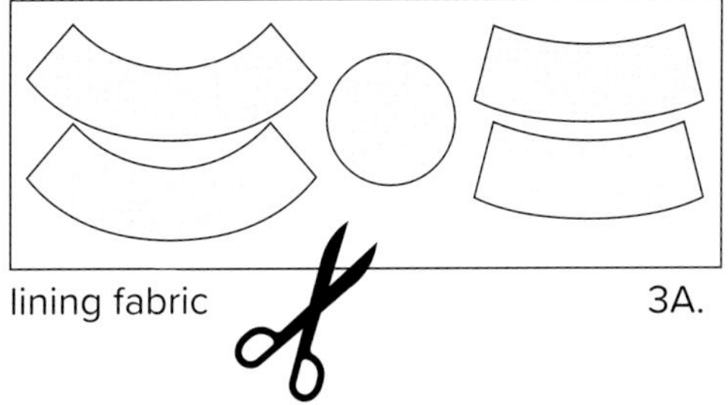

A. From the lining fabric cut out one hat top, two crown, and two brim pattern pieces following the cutting diagram to the right. We will now refer to these as the "lining" pattern pieces.

4. Prepare and attach crown

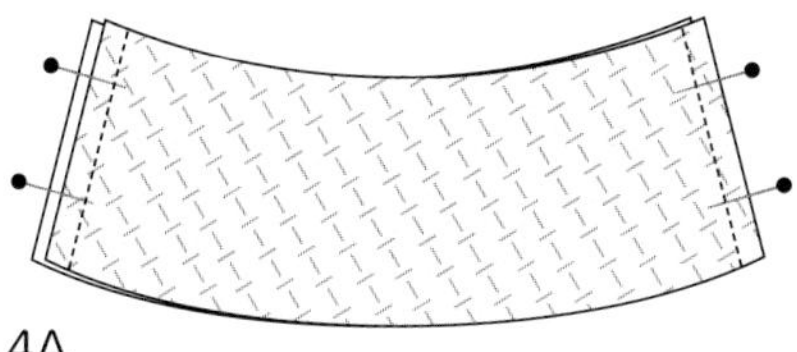

A. With right sides together, align exterior crown side seams. Sew with a ½-inch (1.3cm) seam allowance. Press seams open. Repeat for crown lining panels.

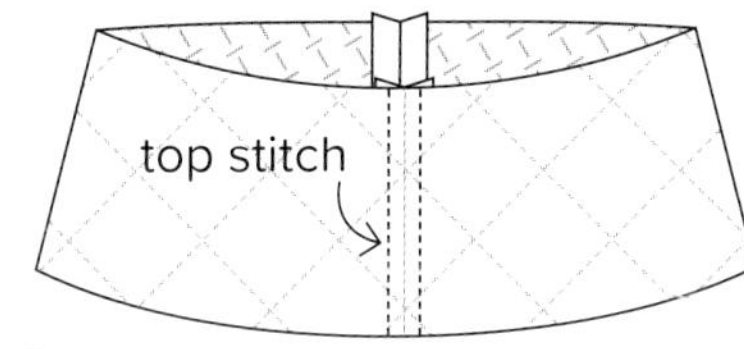

B. From the right side, top stitch ¼ inch (0.6cm) on either side of both side seams, making sure to catch all the seam allowances beneath. Do this for the exterior crown only. The lining crown does not require top stitching.

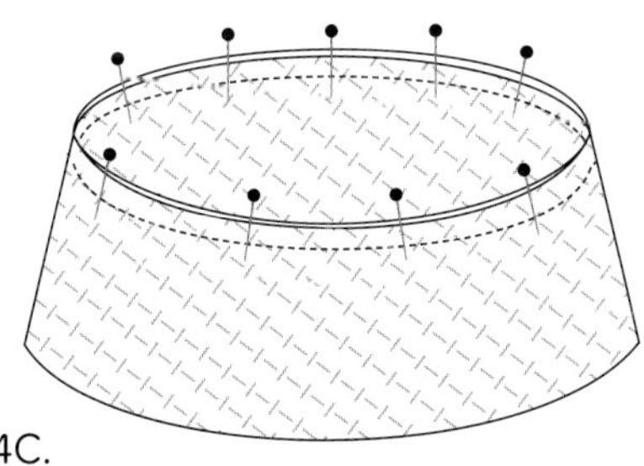

C. With right sides together, ease into place the exterior hat top with top of exterior crown, matching at notches. Two notches will match the side seams, and the remaining two notches will match center notches on crown. Pin in place and sew with a ½-inch (1.3cm) seam allowance. Press seams toward crown. Repeat this same step for the lining pieces.

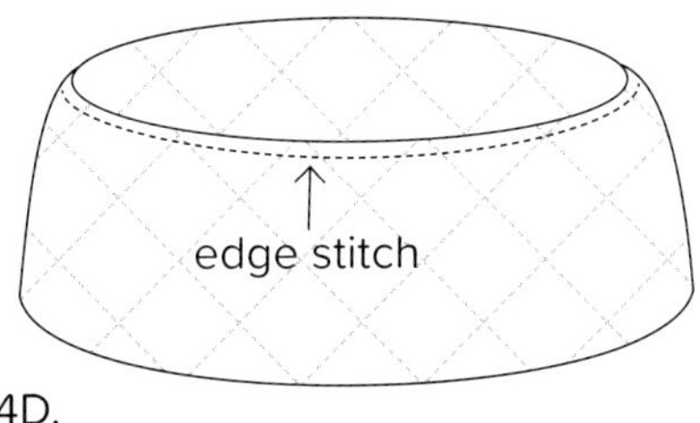

D. From the right side edge, stitch using a ⅛-inch (0.3cm) seam allowance on the exterior crown side, making sure to catch all the seam allowances beneath. The lining piece does not require edge stitching. We will now refer to this as the "exterior upper panel." Set exterior upper panel aside to use in a later step.

5. Prepare brim

A. Follow steps 4A–4B to sew the exterior brim and lining brim.

B. With exterior brim turned right side out and lining brim turned wrong side out, slide exterior brim into lining brim. The right side of exterior brim will now be touching the right side of lining brim.

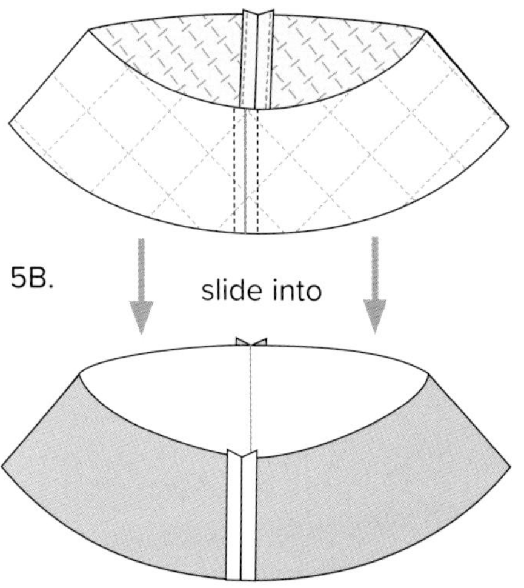

C. Align the side seams and bottom edge. Pin along the bottom edge. Sew with a ½-inch (1.3cm) seam allowance.

D. Flip brim to face the right side. Press in place, making sure the lining does not show from the front. Edge stitch using a ⅛-inch (0.3cm) seam allowance around entire bottom edge. Temporarily secure top edge of brim with a basting stitch using a ¼-inch (0.6cm) seam allowance.

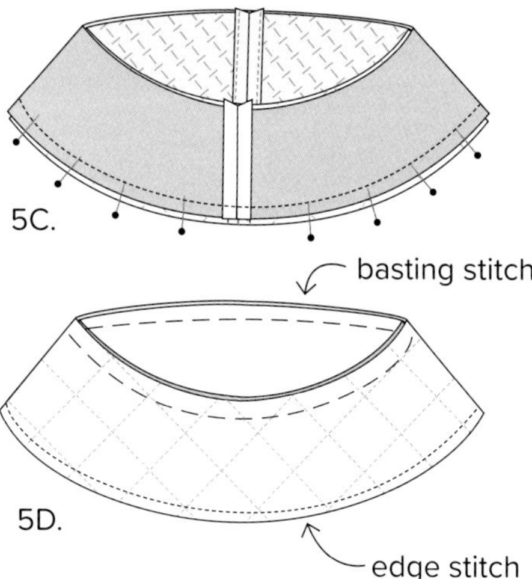

6. Attach ties

A. With the interior side of brim facing out, center raw edge of tie to the side seam. The ties will be touching the interior side of brim. Pin in place. Temporarily secure with a basting stitch using a ¼-inch (0.6cm) seam allowance. Repeat for other tie on opposite side seam. Make sure the tail points of ties are facing the same direction.

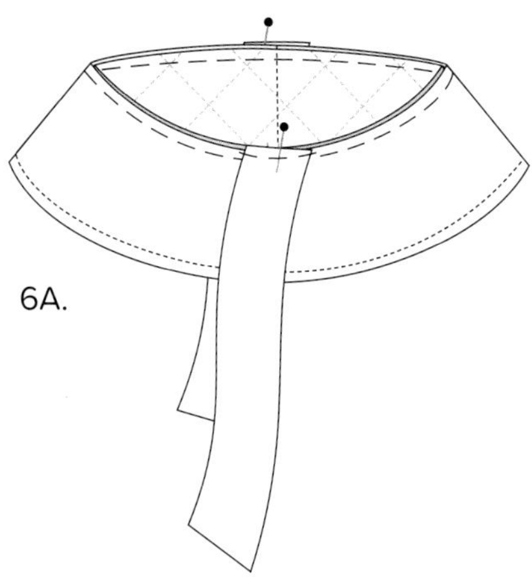

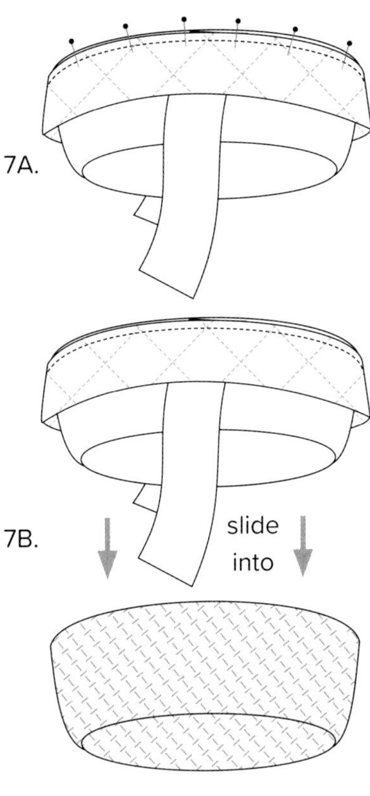

7. Attach brim to crown

A. First attach crown lining to brim. With the right side of crown lining facing the interior side of brim, align the raw edge of crown lining to the raw basted edges of brim. The ties will be facing down and sandwiched between the brim and the crown lining. Pin in place. Sew with a 3/8-inch (1cm) seam allowance.

B. Take the exterior upper panel completed in step 4D and flip so that the wrong side (batting side) faces out. Slide the crown lining with brim and ties attached into the exterior upper panel. Align at side seams. The brim and the ties will be sandwiched in between the crown lining and the exterior upper panel.

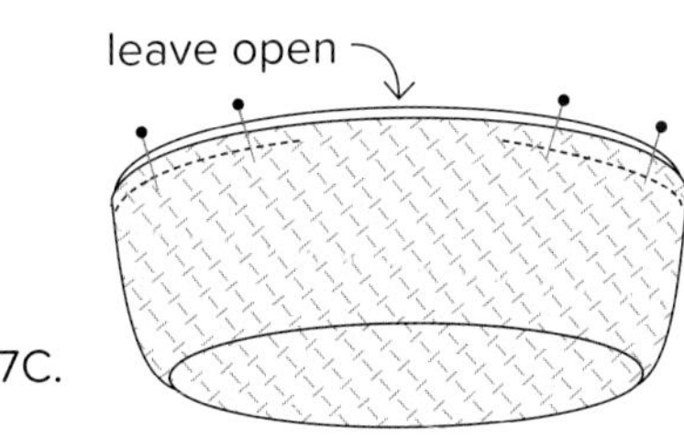

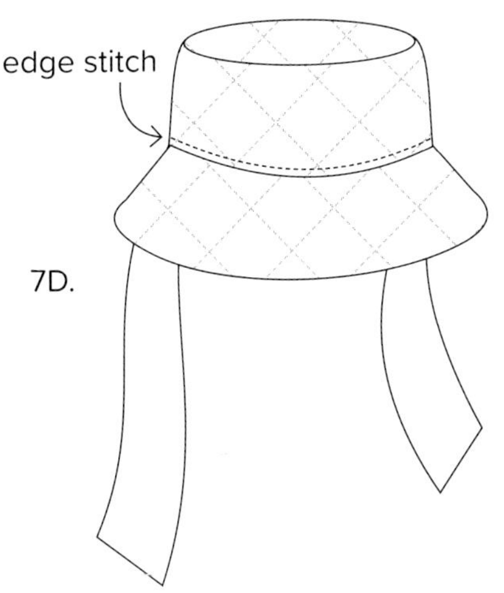

C. Pin in place. Sew with a ½-inch (1.3cm) seam allowance leaving a 4-inch (10cm) opening for turning your hat right side out. Press seam toward crown.

D. Flip hat and ties to the right side using the opening made in step 7C. Tuck in the raw edges from opening using the ½-inch (1.3cm) seam allowance as a guide. Pin opening closed. From the right side of hat, edge stitch using a ⅛-inch (0.3cm) seam allowance on the crown side, closing the opening in the process.

Temporarily pin ties to brim to keep them out of the way while edge stitching.

MARKET DRESS

The Market Dress is the perfect throw-on dress for all outings, mundane and fancy alike!

Shape and Style

Casual and easy to wear, featuring a front slit with neck tie closure.

Fit

Loose with dropped shoulders, puff sleeves, and adjustable length.

Construction

Easy shapes with fun accent incorporating details.

Design Philosophy

Lots of volume paired with a simple bodice create balance and visual play.

Skill level: Advanced beginner

Techniques: Puff sleeves, bias binding with tails, gathering

Fabric suggestions: Lightweight wovens such as linens or cottons

Notions: Coordinating thread

Finished garment measurements (inch/cm)

	XXS	XS	S	M	L	XL
Chest	41½ (106)	43½ (110.5)	45½ (115.5)	47½ (121)	50 (127)	53 (135)
Hip/ Hem	65 (165)	68 (173)	71 (180)	74 (188)	78 (198)	82 (208)

	2XL	3XL	4XL	5XL	6XL
Chest	57 (145)	61 (155)	65 (165)	69 (175)	73 (185)
Hip/ Hem	88 (224)	94 (239)	100 (254)	106 (269)	112 (285)

Total fabric requirements (yard/m) Extra fabric may be needed to match stripes, plaids, or directional prints.

	Length (yard/m)					
Width	XXS	XS	S	M	L	XL
44in 112cm	4 3.7	4 3.7	4 3.7	4¼ 3.9	5¾ 5.3	5¾ 5.3
54in 137cm	3¾ 3.5	3¾ 3.5	3¾ 3.5	4¼ 3.9	4¾ 4.4	4¾ 4.4

Width	2XL	3XL	4XL	5XL	6XL
44in 112cm	5¾ 5.3	5¾ 5.3	5¾ 5.3	5¾ 5.3	5¾ 5.3
54in 137cm	4¾ 4.4	4¾ 4.4	5½ 5.1	5½ 5.1	5½ 5.1

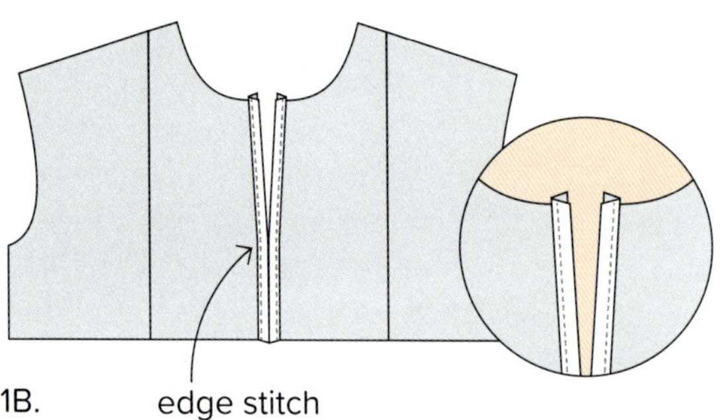

1B.

1. Prepare bodice

A. The Market Dress and Gallery Shirt share the same bodice, with the exception that the Market Dress does not have an extra tie. Follow the same method from the Gallery Shirt instructions on page 116, using steps 1–3. Skip step 4 because the dress does not have the extra tie.

B. Edge stitch on the folded edge from neck to hem. Continue with step 5 from the Gallery Shirt instructions on page 120 to attach shoulder seams.

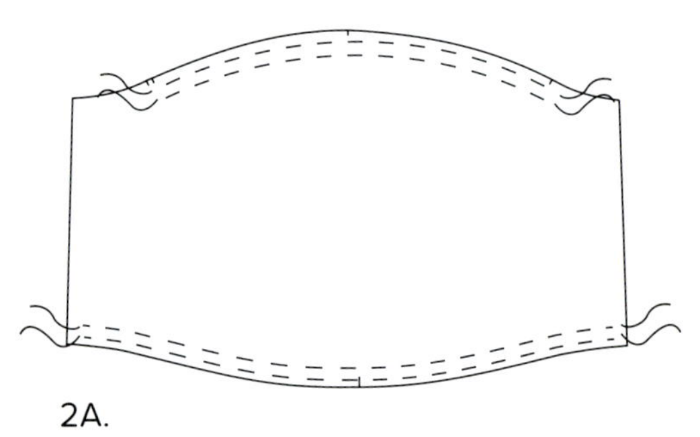
2A.

2. Gather sleeves

A. Gather the top edge of sleeve between notches. Gather the bottom edge, starting and stopping ¾ inch (2cm) away from either side. Follow instructions on page 39 on how to gather.

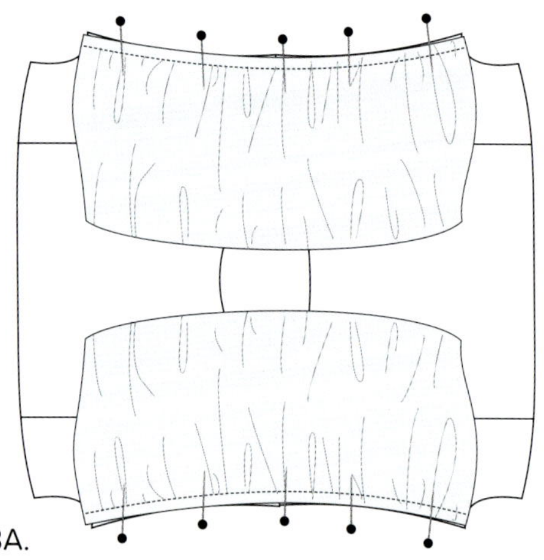
3A.

3. Attach sleeves

A. With right sides together, align the sleeve cap to the armhole, matching at notches. Center notch will align with shoulder seam. Evenly distribute gathers and pin in place. Sew with a ½-inch (1.3cm) seam allowance. Remove this set of gathering stitches **(do not remove gathering stitches at cuff)**. Finish seam with a zigzag stitch or serger. Press seam toward the body. Repeat for other sleeve.

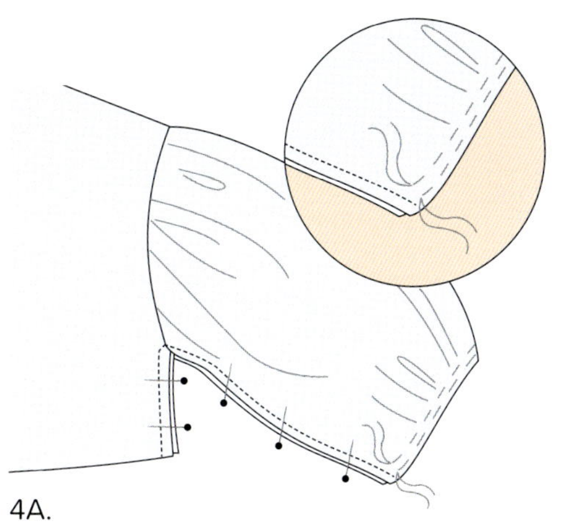
4A.

4. Sew side seams

A. With right sides together, match front and back side seams, aligning at underarm seam. Sew with a ½-inch (1.3cm) seam allowance. Avoid stitching over gathering stitches at cuff. Finish seam with a zigzag stitch or serger. Press seam toward back. Repeat for other side.

5. Prepare and attach sleeve band

A. Cut two sleeve bands according to the measurement chart below. Press to crease the sleeve band as you would for bias binding step 3, shown on page 31.

Band length **x 1¾ inches (4.5cm) high**

	XXS	XS	S	M	L	XL
IN	11½	12	12½	13	13½	14
CM	29.3	30.5	31.8	33	34.3	35.5
	2XL	3XL	4XL	5XL	6XL	
IN	14½	15	15½	16	16½	
CM	37	38	39.5	40.5	42	

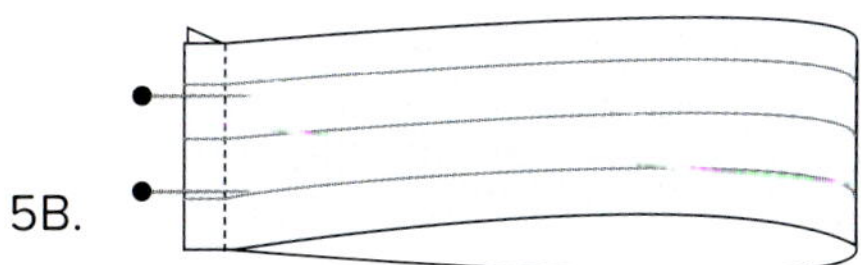
5B.

B. With right sides together, pin short ends of band and sew with a ½-inch (1.3cm) seam allowance, creating a small loop. Press seam open.

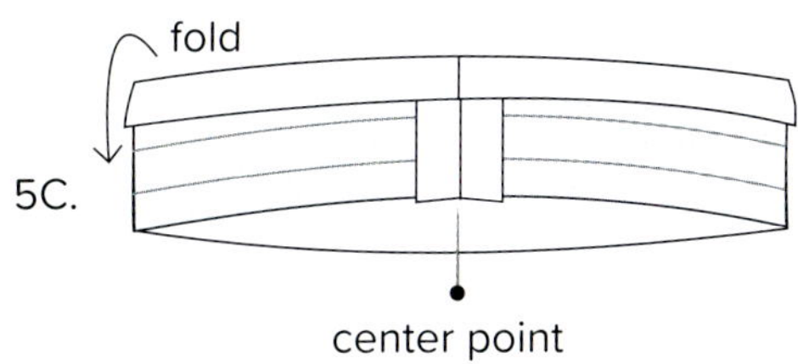

5C.

C. Using the top press line as a guide, fold the top edge of sleeve band ⅜ inch (1cm) toward the wrong side, press in place. The center point of the sleeve band will be directly across from the seam line. Mark this point with a pin. Repeat all steps for both sleeve bands.

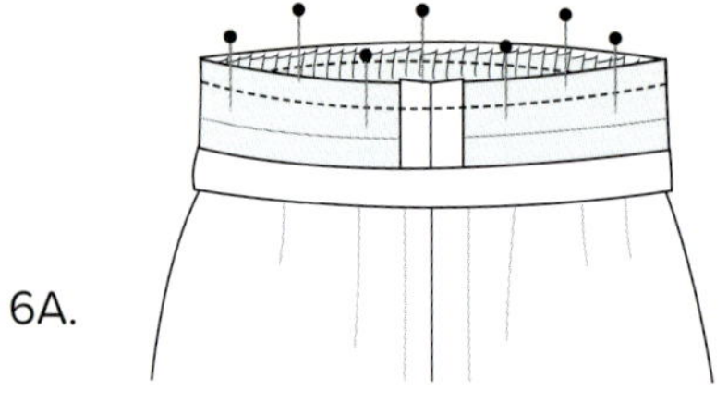
6A.

6. Attach sleeve band

A. With right sides together, align gathered edge of sleeve to raw edge of band, matching at seams and center notch. Distribute gathers evenly and pin in place. Using the upper press line as a guide, sew with a ⅜-inch (1cm) seam allowance. Remove visible gathering stitches.

B. Press sleeve band and seam allowances up and away from sleeve.

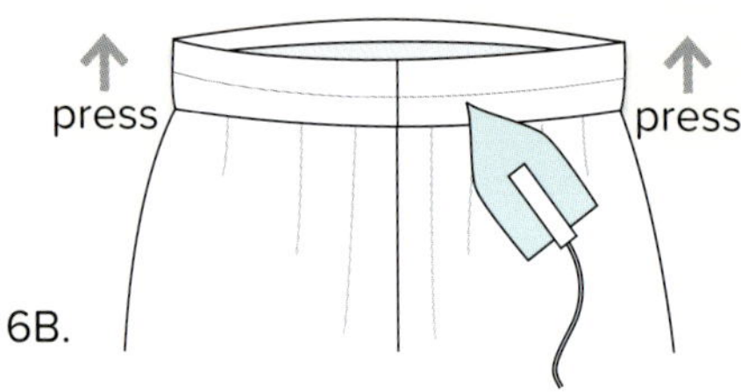

6B.

This area can be bulky—trim seam allowances slightly to make folding band over easier.

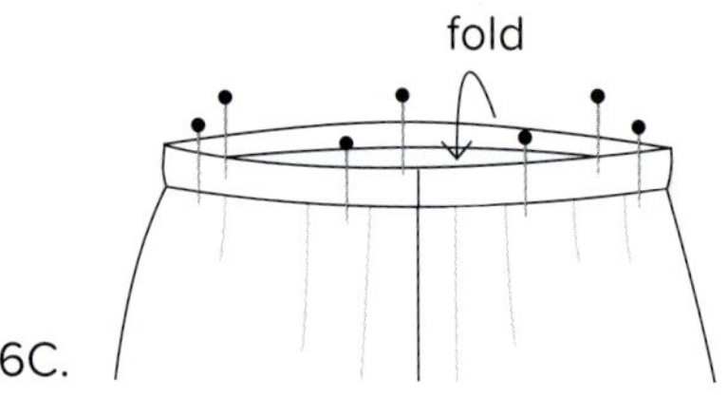

6C.

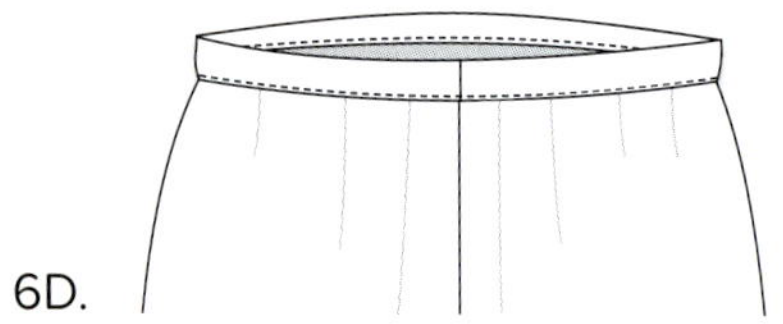
6D.

C. Using the center crease line as a guide, fold sleeve band toward wrong side enclosing all the raw edges and extending just past the stitch line made in step 6A. Pin in place.

D. Working from the right side of the garment, edge stitch where sleeve band meets the sleeve using a "minimal" seam allowance. Make sure to catch the folded edge of sleeve band that is on wrong side of garment. Repeat for other sleeve.

COLOR STRATEGY
ALL THE THINGS

MARKET DRESS

Tip

Patchwork is full freedom of expression, so play, practice, and have fun!

Why it works

This dress is pure patchwork play using fabric from our stash. It's experimental, artistic, and a reminder that you don't always have to follow a strict color strategy. Sometimes your instincts know best. That said, you'll still spot elements that create harmony: yellow, green, and lavender form a subtle triangle on the color wheel with a mix of light and dark values. Patterns are sprinkled throughout, and the contrast is balanced across the garment, keeping the eye moving.

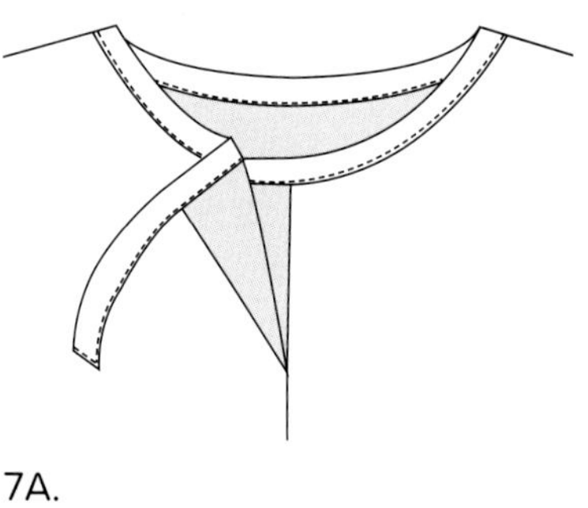

7A.

7. Attach neckline bias binding

A. Cut one length of bias according to the measurement chart below. Continue by following the bias binding with tails method on page 34.

Neckline bias length **x 1⅝ inches (4cm) high**

	XXS	XS	S	M	L	XL
IN	47½	48½	49¼	50	50¾	51½
CM	120.7	123.3	125	127	129	131
	2XL	3XL	4XL	5XL	6XL	
IN	52¼	53	53¾	54½	55¼	
CM	132.7	134.5	136.5	138.5	140.5	

Skirt width **x 34 inches (86.5cm) high**

	XXS	XS	S	M	L	XL
IN	33½	35	36½	38	40	42
CM	85	89	92.7	96.5	101.5	106.7
	2XL	3XL	4XL	5XL	6XL	
IN	45	48	51	54	57	
CM	114.3	122	129.5	137	144.8	

For fuller skirts, add width. For longer or shorter skirts, add or reduce length.

8. Prepare skirt panels

A. Piece together fabric scraps or use a single piece of fabric. Cut final fabric piece to meet the measurement in the chart to the left. You will need two pieces of fabric this size.

B. To find center point of skirt refer to step 4A of Swing Tank instructions (see page 110).

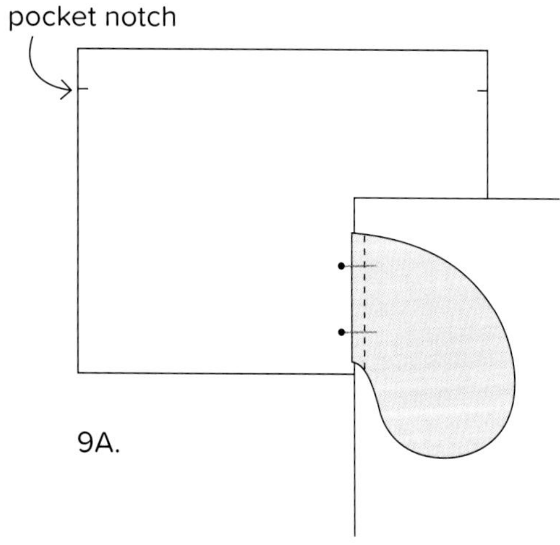

9A.

9. Attach inseam pockets to skirt panels

A. To find pocket notch placement, measure 1 inch (2.5cm) down from top of skirt panel on both side seams for front and back skirt panels. Make a small notch. Continue by following directions for attaching inseam pockets on page 43.

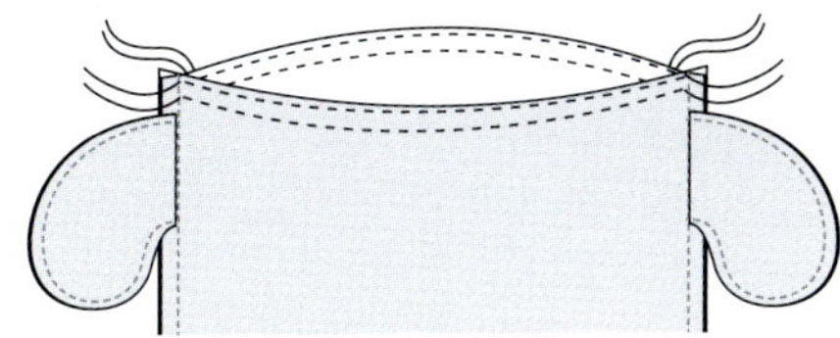
10A.

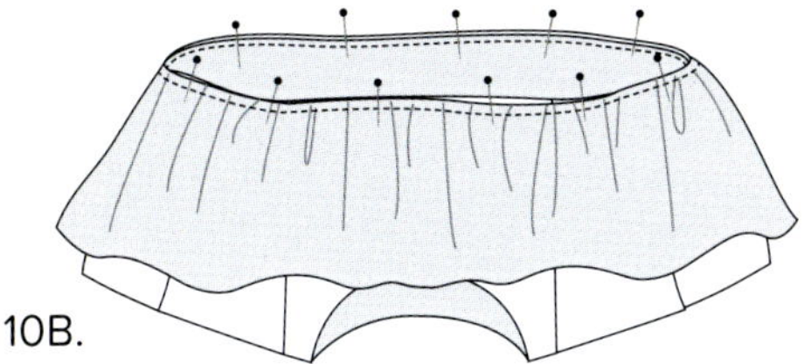
10B.

11A.

10. Gather and attach skirt

A. Your front and back skirt panels are now connected with the inseam pockets attached. Continue by following instructions on page 39 on how to gather. Gather front and back skirt separately, starting and stopping just before the side seams.

B. Continue to attach the skirt by following step 10C from the Gallery Shirt project (see page 122).

11. Hem skirt

A. Fold bottom hem ½ inch (1.3cm) toward wrong side. Press in place. Fold again by another ½ inch (1.3cm). Press and pin in place. Sew ⅛ inch (0.3cm) away from the folded edge.

For details on hemming see page 40.

GLOSSARY

Backstitch
A reverse stitch commonly used to secure the stitches at the beginning and end of a seam.

Basting
Temporary, long stitches used to hold fabric pieces together before the final sewing.

Batting
The layer of insulation between the quilt top and back of your quilt.

Bias
The diagonal grain of a fabric, which has stretch and is often used for binding edges. Bias tape is a strip of fabric cut on the bias and used to bind edges.

Bobbin
A small spool that holds the lower thread in a sewing machine.

Dart
A V-shaped, tapered tuck that shapes a garment to fit the curves of the body.

Drape
The way a fabric hangs when it's left to its own weight.

Ease
The amount of room in a garment that allows for comfortable movement; it prevents garments from feeling too tight.

Easing
Sewing two fabric pieces of different lengths together by slightly gathering the longer one to match the length of the shorter one.

Edge stitch
A row of stitching on the very edge of a garment.

Facing
Fabric used on the inside of a garment to finish the edges, such as necklines or armholes.

Gathering
The process of pulling fabric along a line of stitching to create soft folds.

Grainline
Describes the direction of the warp (lengthwise) and the weft (widthwise) threads in a woven fabric.

Hem
The edge of a piece of fabric that is folded up and sewn, usually at the bottom of a garment.

Hera marker
A small, handheld tool used to crease fabric.

Interfacing
A material used to add stiffness or structure to parts of garments, like collars or cuffs.

Notch

Small marks or cuts, typically no longer than ¼ inch (0.6cm), used to ensure pieces are aligned correctly. A double notch typically indicates the back of a pattern piece.

Placket

A finished opening in a garment that allows the wearer to put it on and take it off more easily.

Pleat

A fold in fabric that is fixed in place, used to add fullness or create decorative effects.

Presser foot

The part of the sewing machine that holds fabric down as it is sewn.

Quilting

The process of joining multiple layers of fabric together by manual stitching or machine.

Rotary cutter

A handheld tool with a circular blade for cutting fabric.

Seam allowance

The space between the edge of the fabric and the line of stitches, usually ¼–⅝ inch (0.6–1.5cm).

Selvage

The tightly woven side edge of a length of fabric that prevents it from unraveling and is used to identify fabric grain.

Serger

A specialized sewing machine that uses multiple threads to sew fabric together, trim the edges, and finish raw edges to prevent fraying in one sewing motion.

Staystitch

A line of stitching sewn through a single layer to help prevent the fabric from stretching and distorting.

Straight grain

The direction of the threads running parallel to the selvage.

Tension

The adjustment that ensures the sewing machine produces a balanced stitch without puckering.

Top stitch

A decorative and/or functional line of stitching sewn close to the edge of a seam.

Under stitch

A row of stitching used to keep facings or seams from rolling to the outside of a garment.

Zigzag stitch

A machine stitch that produces a zigzag pattern, used for stitching stretchable fabrics or finishing edges to prevent fraying.

INDEX

ACKNOWLEDGMENTS

To the Matchy Matchy sewing community. Leaping from a fun hobby to an actual business, and writing a book, in the span of a few years is mind-boggling. It's all due to the sewists who make truly above and beyond garments from our patterns. We envision Matchy as a place where everyone is welcome and anything goes. From the very beginning, you've got us. The online sewing community has offered invaluable encouragement, support, and feedback. We are forever in your debt. A special thank-you to Rebecca, who has tested each pattern in this book (and almost every other Matchy pattern) with a discerning eye and impeccable sense of style.

To our small and mighty support team for your help in all the ways we need it most. Jackie and Terrie for keeping us on track and getting orders shipped. Chelsea and Morgan for being the most gracious models, you make us look like we know what we're doing.

To our team at Quarto—Anna, Ella, and Martina—for holding our hands through this entire process and all of your enthusiasm along the way. It's been so lovely to work with a team of women who love their work. You've made our work shine, too.

Finally, to our families. For putting up with us and the perpetual accumulation of fabric in the name of "research." For carrying heavy things and not batting an eye at our unhinged ideas. You're the real heroes.